D0913169

THE PERSON-IN-DISTRESS

Psychiatry Series

Retreat from Sanity: The Structure of Emerging Psychosis
M.B. Bowers, Jr., M.D.

Strategic Intervention in Schizophrenia: Current Developments in Treatment
R. Cancro, M.D. et al

The Behavioral Treatment of Psychotic Illness: Advances in Theory and Technique
W. DiScipio, Ph.D.

Overload: The New Human Condition
L. Bellak, M.D.

Psychiatry in Broad Perspective
R.R. Grinker, Sr., M.D.

The Person in Distress: On the Biosocial Dynamics of Adaptation
N. Hansell, M.D.

International Directory of Psychiatrists and Mental Hospitals
E.N. Rogan, Ph.D.

Long-Term Treatments of Psychotic States
C. Chiland, M.D.

The Psychotic Animal: A Psychiatrist's Study of Human Delusion
W.J. Garre, M.D.

THE PERSON-IN-DISTRESS
On the Biosocial Dynamics of Adaptation

Norris Hansell IV, M.D., M.S. Hyg.

Professor of Psychiatry
The Medical School
Northwestern University
Chicago, Illinois

Lecturer in Psychiatry
Laboratory of Community Psychiatry
Harvard Medical School
Boston, Massachusetts

HUMAN SCIENCES PRESS
SUBSIDIARY OF BEHAVIORAL PUBLICATIONS INC.
72 FIFTH AVENUE, NEW YORK, N.Y. 10011   (212) 243-6000

Library of Congress Catalog Number 74-8096
ISBN: 0-87705-213-1
Copyright © 1976 by Behavioral Publications, Inc.

BEHAVIORAL PUBLICATIONS, INC.
72 Fifth Avenue
New York, New York 10011

Printed in the United States of America
   89   98765432

Library of Congress Cataloging in Publication Data

Hansell, Norris.
      The person-in-distress.

      Includes bibliographical references.
      1. Helping behavior.   2. Adaptability (Psychology)
I. Title. [DNLM: 1. Psychiatry. WM100 H249p 1974]
RC480.5.H28   616.8'914   74-8096

To Margaret

CONTENTS

Introduction: About Helping

We all offer it. We all accept it. One of man's oldest journeys is the movement along the path from solitude to the presence, and aid, of fellow travelers. That a cry in the night will yield to an embrace. That he who offers his hand to one in peril forms a link in a chain which many may use.

This is a book about people-in-trouble, helpers and helping. It is a book of observations that surprised me, as the idea etched its mark that "helping" persons-in-distress can involve activities that elude obvious description. The whole of this book engages with the perplexing situation that many who regularly help others cannot say what they do. Further, that some who speak with confidence about helping are, in the accomplishment, less impressive. These essays occasionally stumble into the mystery of how it could come to be that some of those who have taken "full time" helping roles, stride their paths paying little heed to the prior fabric of which they are part.

The domain of activity created by the interaction of people-in-trouble and the persons surrounding them has often been pieceworked in fine detail, as if the major questions—biological, psychological, sociological—had been faced. Part of the reason why untested belief in this field retains such a strong influence may proceed from the fact that every person has acquired a body of personal, direct experience in the subject, an experience formed within his own cultural instructions and energized in human biology. And the clarioned mazeway governing the interactions around a person-in-distress has sometimes operated to confine a curiosity that might otherwise easily have detected several simple principles.

This book is addressed to a broad group of thoughtful people who are increasingly open toward the possibility of a general theory that can form the basis of solid advances in service design. Interest runs high in the helping professions to construct a group of concepts that can resolve the recent flood of explorations in new service patterns into some order. Many workers feel a need for an approach that draws from the biological and social sciences, so as to establish a few axioms with decisive value in constructing a variety of effective services. This book seeks to provide a start toward this need.

With me in this attempt are my colleagues at the H. Douglas Singer Center in Rockford, Illinois, at the Laboratory of Community Psychiatry, Department of Psychiatry, Harvard Medical School, Boston and at the Department of Psychiatry, Northwestern University, Chicago.

We hope that the book will challenge the reader to rearrange some of his human understanding so as to become available to a category of insight he did not know he had. And in all this we ask the sympathy due those who would shatter the cornerstone to construct the wheel.

If this book adds a bit of method to the mysteries of helping, without slowing the heartbeat, we are on the way.

Acknowledgments

This book would not have been possible were it not for the direct assistance of the following persons, and I am pleased to acknowledge my deep gratitude to them: members of the staff of the H. Douglas Singer Zone Center in Rockford, particularly Donald W. Hart, Dr. William G. Smith, Mary Wodarczyk, Dr. Britomar Handlon-Lathrop and the late Marvin L. Benson; Dr. Anthony F. C. Wallace and Dr. Joseph T. English, who assisted in the early formation of several of the concepts; Ruth B. Caplan, who helped me discover historical roots for several basic designs for service; Dr. Bernard Rubin, who taught me a method for understanding the behavior of people in hospitals; my secretaries, Iris Barta, Gwynne Marquardt, Lois Michel, Terri Johnson, and Louise Trefz, who worked on this manuscript with care in the midst of the daily flow of our busy offices; and my wife, Margaret, who gave me valuable guidance for focusing the book on a few main points. From the beginning of this book and the projects it recounts, Dr. Gerald Caplan has been my teacher and good friend. And throughout the whole, Dr. Harold M. Visotsky has helped me see what should be done and develop the courage and resources to do it. I am also grateful to the editors of the *Archives of General Psychiatry* for permission to include in Chapter VII material which they published in 1967, 1968, 1970 and 1971.

N.H.
September 4, 1973

I

THE STATE OF "BEING-IN-DISTRESS"

Could it be that several facts around which our service efforts regularly turn are much the same for many people, and derive from commonalities in each situation of a "being-in-distress?" What are the general forces that govern, and the norms attendant on this discrete social domain? Could some of our earlier service efforts have gotten sidetracked into dealing with differences in detail regarding persons-in-distress because we have overlooked several omnipresent, fundamental facts staring us in the face? As we move into the planning of the service problems we have undertaken here, let us organize our responses to deal first with the factors that persons-in-distress—and the people that surround them —share in common during episodes of profound upheaval. Let it be our purpose to assist individuals, families and groups as they work to manage their states of "being-in-distress." Let us also attempt to assist these persons in a manner that may prepare them to make headway in the continuing hard work of facing life's flow of adaptive challenges.

Persons faced with episodes of unusual adaptive challenge show a set of behaviors which, taken together, comprise a major dynamic governing what others can do that

*will work as helpful service; specifically, the crisis picture
includes a characteristic pattern of attention, identity, affectional attachments, memory, role performance, decision
making and distress signaling.*

Much of the behavior expressed during a profound crisis
interval is common to all persons experiencing such an interval, whatever the cause of the crisis may be. We can use the
term "crisis" to designate any rapid change or type of encounter which is very much outside a person's usual range of
experience. A situation is problematically "different" in this
sense when it does not stimulate a person to handle, or directively react, to it. It does not call forth ready responses. Consider the range of challenges which can "stress" a being—
loss of a beloved person or situation, transposition in geographic space, loss of health, loss of a limb, loss of a life
objective or ideal, catastrophes of flood and weather, and the
social catastrophes of unemployment, war and pestilence.
All are situations calling for novel or rapid personal change.
All are situations that place persons into the experience and
predicament of crisis, as well as putting life and personality
at risk.

Let us make some observations of this crisis behavior,
all the while trying to keep our observations focused on cri-
sis-as-such, silhouetted against a background situation that
may vary greatly from one case to the next. What can we see
that could be considered as part of a "standard package" of
crisis behavior, or "crisis plumage?" If we can detect such a
regular phenomenon, we may decide to use it as a marker of
crisis. We may decide to detect it and then quickly "place it
aside," so as to proceed with other work. It might be helpful,
for instance, to be able to "see through" the regular behavior
of crisis so as to be free to work on the task of "detecting
personality." Let us try to become so familiar with any regularities in crisis behavior that we can use them to detect, to
mark, to bugle, that a person is in-trouble. Let us use the
presentation of a person displaying "crisis plumage" to signal an occasion when a person is wrestling with a radical,

adaptive challenge. The availability of such a marker will help us with the questions of "when" and "who" in our services.

SOME REGULARITIES IN CRISIS

1. *The individual shows a narrowed, fixed span of attention.* He is not scanning his entire environment, but is focused down on a few items. He may ruminate on a few details of a complex situation. The attention is fixed, or frozen, for intervals of minutes, constrained from its usual flow through a sequence of organized thought. It also jumps around without any strategy of "scanning." The narrowed, constricted pattern of attention during distress is a liability, because it displaces a more ordinary, and vital, pattern. A flowing, systematic scan of the environment, linked with the ability to "stick with" a new fact, and "work on" it, is a major engine of adaptivity. Whereas ordinarily a person rearranges thoughts until he generates an action which will work, during a crisis his thought gets "stuck." Common instances of such "cycling" in thought would be notions like, "I am helpless," "I am incompetent," "People are after me," "My life is no good," or "I'm a victim of some circumstances." As we observe him, the individual seems to be preoccupied. He may also press upon the listener a "topic of choice." "Topic of choice" and fixity of attention are two views of the same process, a reduction in the scanning activity of attention. We may also be struck by the fact that the person adheres to fixed sentiments, or affects, such as suspicion or sadness. Sometimes the topic centers on a set of complaints, perhaps complaints about many people in the environment. The fixity of thinking is often associated with feelings of being generally, or totally, helpless. Sometimes the fixed notion can be a recurrent impulse to act, or "to do something." Such fixed notions can include impulses to hurt the self, as in suicide, or to flee the scene. Such repetitive, fixed notions to act often include carelessly constructed reasoning. There are very pressing notions of some-

thing "that must be done," which have very little relation-ship to the individual's prior thought or experience. These characteristic findings of narrowed, fixed attention, with ac-companying fixed feelings and notions for action, are part of our basic planning facts for developing a strategy of help. They are basic to constructing a plan because they mark sit-uations of overwhelming distress, and because the cessation of the scanning function of attention interferes with essen-tial, problem-solving work.

2. *The individual shows "loosening" and "widening" of his affectional attachments.* His "social connections," his stable patterns of activity directed toward persons, groups, fam-ilies and projects, show a characteristic decay of precision and pattern. Normally there is a regularity to the distribu-tion of an individual's sentiments and interests. He focuses his energies and activity onto particular people, groups, and projects. Such focusing binds an individual into a matrix of affections, or social attachments. While ordinarily such in-terests structure and "connect" a person, during crisis such attachments become weak or intermittent. As the patterning of socially directed activity breaks down, persons report feeling "separated," "distant" or "unhooked." We are not con-cerned, when we assess events at crisis, whether the loos-ened attachments are of ones of love, hate, suspicion or trust. Such an inquiry is very much a second order of concern at the point of crisis. Rather, we must reckon the status of pri-mary, vital moorings to social objects in the environment, with the purpose of identifying such objects and the integ-rity of the corresponding attachments.

Of equal importance during crisis is the extraordinary activation of those behaviors that initiate new attachments. Especially prominent are behaviors like moving up close, seeking eye and skin contact and offering unguarded, inti-mate language—all behaviors which are part of sequences to "reach out" for new attachments. If often appears that, coin-cident with the decline in older, regular attachments, the in-dividual develops a random, migratory "search and attach" pattern. The person feels, acts and signals as if in readiness to "latch on and hold." People who work in clinical settings that receive many individuals-in-distress have abundant experience with this urgent, diffuse attachment behavior. Clinicians experienced in reception work often report a "clutchy," "clingy," "demanding" component regularly present in the behavior of people in profound trouble. Such persons appear to want to attach to anyone immediately present or to anyone willing to respond. It may be useful for clinicians to remind themselves that such crisis-linked attachment movements do not arise so much because clinicians are peculiarly attractive as persons, as because clinicians are particularly likely to be *present* during the critical time that an individual is passing through a crisis interval. To an individual experiencing a critical level of terror, any person with a temperature of 98.6° may appear to comprise a satisfactory attachment opportunity. It is less an organized choice than a mooring in panic.

There is, then, at crisis, an altered distribution of affectional activity. The individual is deploying a more "randomized" attachment behavior. And random attachments can be risky. Latching onto those who may be handy sidesteps all the precision built into ordinary approaches. Linkages can occur with persons who may be exploitive, or have little interest in reciprocal, continuing activities.

The heightened attachment activity in crisis has particularly profound consequences for individuals who are, in their normal context, social isolates. Persons who are beset with a crisis, and are without available family or friends, are often caught in a random, accidental, social context. Sometimes they are exclusively among "treatment people," who, whatever skills they may have, lack direct knowledge of the individual's personality or previous performance. The peculiarly risky position of isolated persons who are passing through an adaptational crisis is one of the central problems of clinical practice. Isolated people, during crisis, are set in a social field which can only perceive their current, atypical, unattractive behavior. Consequently they can direct their attachment energies only toward people who are either temporary or "strangers." Later, we will approach this problem using what we have gained from defining its origins.

But for all persons, isolated or not, the exquisitely heightened activity of the affectional attachments during crises dominates much of what transpires. One prime result is that many persons who contact treatment systems during crises latch onto the people and settings they encounter. All too often, the service activities recruit troubled people quite securely into continuing linkage with social networks which might better have done their work well and bade "farewell." The tendency for distressed persons to become separated from their regular networks and life-styles and transferred into the treatment networks emerges as a catastrophic hazard of service. The degree of hazard probably can be raised or lowered by aspects of service activity. Particularly hazardous are ideologies which encourage professional helpers to send signals inviting their clients into shelter or asylum. Practices emanating from notions describing "bad families," "schizophrenogenic mothers," and "toxic environments," often appear to convey promissory notes for shelter. And notes offering shelter are every bit as interesting to persons-in-distress as are mirages to weary desert travelers. The loosened and randomized attachment activity at crisis can just as well lead to improved friendships as to asylum, and we shall have more to say about this later.

3. *The individual-in-distress experiences a profound loss of moorings to a clear vision of his identity.* Normally, people can experience, when they so desire, clear notions of an identity. Most of the time, people can summon a defining set of impressions of who they are, and of what capacities and skills they demonstrate. Such notions sort and simplify incoming experience. The definition of experience is a basal step in making decisions and taking effective action. However, during the period of crisis the personal experience of identity becomes diffused, vague and volatile. The individual seems unaware of who he is. He shows difficulty in telling

about his regular experiences and satisfactions. In crisis, therefore, the individual is "set afloat." Not only does this result in the discomfort that accompanies a loss of orienting notions about the self; individuals also appear stranded, without a map of the possibilities, or else flailing with precipitate action.

The loss of the experience of identity brings more risks than those of indecision. Individuals-in-crisis are exquisitely tuned in to pick up signals coming to them from the surrounding social field about who they are and what they should do. Persons-in-trouble quite often seem to play out a drama, which can last for years, using identities and roles taken up quickly at crisis. When a person does not know who he is, those who appear to tell him acquire a capacity to create an identity for him, to select one out of ambiguity. *During crisis, an individual's identity lies substantially in the social surround.* A person is vulnerable, in crisis, not just to what can happen to him, but to the effects of what he can decide is true about himself. The achievement of clarity in the experience of self, wrested out of a dark, chaotic flood, can bring a comfort that is sometimes achieved at the cost of personal constriction. It is often tempting to reach a comforting definition based either on ceasing to strive for previous values, or on the "received" sense of oneself as incapable.

The social surround, especially one that knows and cherishes a person, carries on functions vital to adaptive work in crisis. The network "remembers" a person's identity and can define away current chaos. Also, the network, knowing his capacity, can detect it when only visible in traces. By recalling a vision of his more usual self, the network acts to "reconvert" a person-in-distress to that usual self. This stabilizing reconversion is one of the main helping activities of friends during the crisis interval. The usual presence and activity of a cherishing social network explains why, although an individual is vulnerable to assuming many different types of identity, he usually is recruited toward a close resemblance of his historical self. The stabilizing effect which social networks have on the personal chaos of crisis is one of the dominant dynamics at crisis. Important roots of friend-ship, conversion and adaptational growth reside in the per-ceptions and expectations of those persons who happen to surround an individual journeying a challenge.

He who is isolated, as well as in chaos, is even more a prisoner of the expectations of his social surround. His situa-tion goes well beyond the pain of loneliness and the despair of anomie. The isolated person is without either his own recollections of self or those of his friends. To form an im-pression of self he has only current images. Whereas the members of an individual's regular social network are often in a position to be selectively inattentive to the decayed per-formance of crisis, and to recollect from the past, those per-sons around an isolate can see only the now. Networks fa-miliar with a person quite regularly place a moratorium on judgments based only on unattractive, current performance at crisis. Reflecting on the past, they will say, "George doesn't look good today," or "George is having a bad day." But in the situation of an individual who is migratory, or lives alone in a rooming house, or is "brought in by the po-lice," there is no surround which can recollect a cherishable past. It is out of such a background that accidental networks, having only the now for reference, wreak such havoc, al-though quite without mal-intent. The behavior displayed in crisis can offer only an unrepresentatively deteriorated image of a whole person. And networks without any recol-lections for reference can project only the current, narrow sample of the individual's behavior, a sample often vastly decayed from what he might ordinarily offer. This sequence of events can sometimes convert the transitory behavior of crisis into a stable identity; this danger is, therefore, one of the concerns of professionals serving at crisis. An episode can become a career. What is "seen" is what becomes perma-nent. Professional helpers trained to be vigilant for symp-toms are acting in a situation where the selectivity of their view of a person can have the effect of converting the or-dinarily fleeting physiology of crisis into the identity state-ment of a permanent casualty.

Guideline 1:   Persons passing through crisis in isolation incur the hazard of being converted into a constricted, decayed identity by having only their current, *atypical* behavior as reference for defining the self.

Guideline 2: ' Persons passing through crisis, and receiving help from professionals preoccupied with the plumage of distress, incur the hazard of being converted into an identity that looks much like the professionals' perception of the "main symptoms in this case."

Professionally directed helping acquires a central obligation to detect and protect that identity and personality which may be temporarily obscured by plumage of distress. The task is to hear the signal through the noise.

4. *The individual-in-distress quite regularly shows socially unsatisfactory performance of his roles.* All the usual things that individuals do—as milkmen, mothers, breadwinners, students—employ intricate, patterned behavior. That which an individual is supposed to do each day is well known to him, and partially known to others. A significant fraction of repeating, daily behavior is in service to a cluster of roles which define primary social connections. During a crisis period, role behavior, as well as most other behavior, becomes more random. Patterned role-states decay toward random, unpatterned pieces of behavior. Things an individual might ordinarily do, he doesn't. Things that he would seldom do are more likely to appear in his behavior. A statistical picture would show behavior to be "randomized." Biologically, the biochemistry and physiology supporting a learned, orderly flow of behavior is replaced by a flow of chemicals linked with the "general adaption syndrome." Materials like epinephrine and nor-epinephrine become greatly more concentrated in the environment of nervous tissue. Behaviors associated with patterns that are apparently inborn, and not

learned, such as fear-display, approach-display or combat, become more prominent.

Crisis, considered biologically, seems to be a change-oriented "fluid state" separating longer, more patterned, "steady states." But the decayed appearance of role behavior at crisis, and the other display states that are often present, tend to arouse distancing, combat and vigilance postures in surrounding social networks. Out of behavior that is random or decayed, the social network may perceive hostile or threatening "meaning." From the standpoint of the members of a loosened social surround, presentation of decayed role behavior is often taken to herald a general, permanent loss of competence. The longer the decayed state lasts, the more sectors of behavior are involved, the more the network forgets about the stable past and the more is the network worried. People move from stabilizing recollections like "George does this," or "Mary is that," to destabilizing observations such as "I don't know about George," "He's not doing his job," "He's not carrying out his roles," "He's not a person that I enjoy being with," "He surprises me," "He frightens me." The members of the social surround then move to distance themselves from people and behavior not falling within expectable patterns. Protracted presentations of decayed role behavior fragment a social network, and further disable a person-in-distress. *For professionals, an episode of decayed role behavior is best regarded as an opportunity for new role acquisition, rather than as a sample of what that new role might be.*

For such reasons, helpers have a keen interest in observing reactions of families and networks to the behavior of distressed members. Is the network "moving in" with attitudes of embrace? Or is the network distancing itself from the person and trouble? Sometimes professionals move in to replace a vanishing network—acting to prevent abandonment. Other times they draw an isolated person into professionally sheltered and cloistered spaces, a tradition called "asylum." Because of a very interesting set of problems with life after asylum, professionals are becoming increasingly reluctant to offer it lightly.

Not only does the individual at crisis display decayed versions of his usual role behavior, but he demonstrates an exquisite capacity to acquire new roles, especially roles suggested by people in the crisis environment. This combination of readiness to leave old roles, and ability to move into new ones, forms a substrate for the adaptive possibility available in crisis. But it contains a hazard as well. The *patienthood* role, or its prolongation into the role of social *casualty,* are role options handily taken up by people-in-distress. The use of patienthood is especially accentuated when, during stress, an individual becomes surrounded by people who encourage its use. Every now and again, a professional will make the person assume the patienthood role as a prior condition to offers of assistance.

Later in these discussions, we will consider the patienthood role more fully. For the present, let us just glimpse some of the hazards inherent in imprecise offers of asylum, or of patienthood. The social expectations around patienthood center on the notions of moratorium and convening or drawing people together. That is, the patienthood role-state provides a temporary suspension of, or moratorium on, conventional, social expectations that an individual will perform his usual functions with his ordinary energy, skill or reliability. Along with this projection of temporarily reduced capacity, the role invites the social surround to move into temporary activities of a helping, giving or embracing quality. The arrangements for moratorium and giving are conventional and dutiful and, thus, proceed without loss of dignity or projection of constraints on the individual's right to the regard of his surround. But the feature of temporariness is central to the social properties of the patienthood role. The transit time is ordinarily brief and the role can be considered nothing but an "episode." The intriguing social productivity of the patienthood role seems to reside in the temporizing envelope it can place around episodes of distress. The role can maintain affiliations during episodes when relatedness may be at risk. A distinctly different state of affairs is at hand when this temporary state of affairs is prolonged beyond several days or several weeks. The temporary, moratorium effect becomes converted into a persisting identity and role statement. And the constricted expectations of patienthood are converted from an asset to a morbid liability.

As we proceed with our work, let us keep a close watch on how we use the patienthood role system. Is it essential to link our helping work with regular invitations to patienthood? How frequently will we wish to convey persons into patienthood in order to use services we expect to require months or years? Defined time and defined purpose may be proper guides in the decision to employ the role.

But the expression of our resolve in these areas promises many challenges to our ingenuity. The individual-in-distress will be offering decayed behavior, often greatly out of keeping with his ordinary role requirements. His social surround will be moving away and galvanizing to redefine his roles and status. And beyond this, the person-in-trouble will be signaling us that he is exquisitely ready to become a redefined person.

We will need more than resolve to avoid the hazards of sanctuarial styles of service. Even framing the patienthood role within expectations of short duration will not deal with the observation that distressed persons can learn it very fast. In a situation where a person-in-trouble has no roles to which he is successfully addressed, the patienthood role can appear inviting. Where there is already very little dignity, the status in patienthood is a step up. Where there is little stability to experience, the clarity of the situation in patienthood offers welcomed relief. If our style of service can offer no other stability, dignity and connectedness, save that which attends being a patient, we will surely be inviting use of the crisis interval for sanctuarial rather than adaptational work. The convertibility of role in crisis offers a basis for both opportunity and hazard.

Perhaps we can learn how to offer enlarged, attractive role invitations to individuals tumbling in the anguish of the crisis state. We can expect they will be highly responsive to our signals regarding role and identity projections. If we use the flexibility of crisis to introduce a person to a set of roles useful mainly in a treatment or institutional situation, we will have dropped the ball. When we begin to think about return to ordinary settings, the former, conventional roles may have atrophied. The peculiar role-entrainment vulnerability which attaches to the "role-suspended state" during crisis fixes a heavy responsibility on the helper. Any roles we teach or address even briefly may linger indefinitely to haunt us all.

Guideline 3:   A professional conveyance into patienthood is least hazardous when directed into specific task objectives and a defined transit time. The tasks and work undertaken during use of the role are most adaptive when they serve non-sanctuarial, quite ordinary definitions of identity, status and dignity.

Guideline 4:   The decayed role performance characteristic of the crisis state can serve as a signal for the helping network to invite the individual to entertain a new role or identity. The helpers can assist a person discover what definitions of self he can cherish.

5. *The individual-in-distress experiences an altered state of consciousness which includes a random-access memory.* Normally there are always filters on memory which affect the access of storage to consciousness. Certain areas of prior experience are, at any time, unavailable. The intriguing kind of impact that this unavailable experience can exert on behavior has led to a large literature about "the unconscious." The direction of the filtering action can be of two types. Some aspects of previous experience are, at any moment, filtered *out*, while others are actively selected *into* current awareness. The latter category of memories are experienced as pressing upon attention. These intrusive memories seem obvious and clear. They come into awareness accompanied by affects of certitude and conviction. During the entire interval

when adaptational physiology prevails, the crisis-in-transit period, both "filtering in" and "filtering out" activities are reduced. And resultingly, the flow of memory seems "random." Experiences from the past, normally not available, are brought into view. Other notions, ones which have seemed sharply obvious, no longer even come to mind. This randomizing of the access to memory is similar to the migratory quality of the flow of attention during crisis. And it is similar to the decayed, convertible nature of role behavior, and of affectional attachments during crisis.

Observers become aware that the random-access mode of recall is present as an individual reports his experience with an accompanying perplexity and lack of certitude. The social surround usually finds such a state of mind both interesting and worrisome. Most members of a network usually regard this altered state of consciousness as bizarre. Professional helpers, who have become accustomed to its outlines, and who use it in eliciting change, find it less worrisome. The biologic advantage, or survival value, deriving from occasional episodes of random-access memory during adaptational challenges is most evident when it is linked with the orderly thoughts of another individual, one not in crisis. Perhaps, the basal requirement for the constructive use of crisis is the interaction of a person-in-crisis with a person-not-in-crisis. The productivity of helping roles is rooted in this interaction. The malleability of the random-access memory becomes an asset only when combined with the task-drive of a person focused on problem-solving. The openness of the random-access mode, an openness even to considering the absurd and impossible, becomes coupled to the orderly thoughts of another person. Such a coupling yields a drive to survive by taking action. The special value to survival results from innovation-plus-action, from distress-plus-focus, from random-access-plus-task-drive. As an individual loses some notions about which he has formerly felt certain, the way is open for new, more adaptive action. The flexible cognition of crisis which is linked to the random-access memory is central to many service designs.

6. *The individual-in-distress experiences a drastically re-*
duced ability to make decisions. Decision-making involves
steps of inventory, appraisal, decision, action and review.
And, although it ordinarily proceeds inexorably, like respiration, in profound crisis it meanders falteringly. The readiness at crisis to consider *many* notions, which we discussed
above, is only step one. Equally necessary is the subsequent
act of conferring reality, or verity, to *only some* notions. The
act of deciding entails selecting from among competing mental notions. The aborted, meandering character of decision
work offered by the solitary person-in-crisis is a benchmark
of the crisis-in-transit state. The striking increase in the
ability to decide, and to act, when a second person puts the
special crisis consciousness to work, is equally a benchmark.
The necessity for input by the social surround, in order to
release the potentiality of crisis, is the radical center of de-
signs for service, professional and folk. People-in-distress
bring a readiness for change which does not galvanize into
discrete activity until there is input from persons not in crisis. Activities to provide the corporate substrate for problem-solving form a foundation of many service designs.

Guideline 5: A necessary, but not sufficient, ingredient for
producing the care-giving relationship, is the
approximation, within a close, signaling exchange, of a person-in-crisis and a person *not*
in crisis.

Guideline 6: Growth-promoting types of care-giving activity avoid a focus on chemical or sanctuarial
relief-of-distress, when possible, and aim to
facilitate the work of decision and action.
They work to stimulate emergence of adaptive behavior and to resolve distress by applying its unique potential for reorganization.

7. *Individuals-in-distress send signals of distress.* All the
primates, most mammals that live in colonies, and many oth-

er species, send characteristic distress signals during periods of threat to survival. Such signals alert the group to hazard and mobilize "helping" activity in behalf of the sender of the signals. Distress signals often stimulate "clustering" orientations around the troubled member and, sometimes, cooperative, corporate activity. The cooperative activity is most often an attempt to fix, remove or flee the situation. Distress information among mammals is often transmitted via several channels of signaling—including posture, smell and sound. Humans also use language and role behavior. Members of the same species apparently can quickly recognize each others' distress signals. They appear to have in continuing readiness, learned, as well as unlearned, response attitudes. The general activities called forth in such attitudes are clustering, assessing, embracing, or helping if possible; and extrusion of the signaler, or flight, if no satisfactory response can be developed quickly. Much of our work as professional helpers is related to attempts to modify and orchestrate such built-in responses of humans to signals of distress.

Guideline 7: Knee-jerk reactions to distress signals, for instance the offering of general asylum, or abandonment to solitary demise, are seldom the most effective assists to adaptive work. Nevertheless, a biologically primary readiness to embrace-or-extrude probably underlies more precise "helping" behaviors in us all.

Seven types of behavior at crisis can assist in recognizing, and using for growth, this extraordinary interval of readiness. Characteristic alterations of attention, identity, affectional attachments, memory, role performance, decision-making and distress signaling combine to create a biologically flexible, transition state.

Table 1 reviews the observations given above in abbreviated form.

We are going to assume that the descriptions offered in

Table 1
CHARACTERISTIC BEHAVIOR OF PERSONS AT CRISIS

Aspect of Behavior	Usual Appearance in Crisis
Attention	Migratory, narrowed, fixed A topic-of-choice
Affectional attachments	Loosened, widened, acquisitive
Identity	Diffuse, vague, convertible
Role performance	Decayed, unreliable, convertible
Network attitude	Fragmenting, malleable Readiness to embrace or extrude
Memory	Random access, reduced certitude Flowing "whir and blur"
Decision activity	Halting, meandering Strikingly improved with outside input
Signaling	Distress situation is present Coordinative information to surround

Table 1 are pertinent, and reasonably accurate, as we explore their implications in our designs for service. It may be worth your time, therefore, to construct your own summary of the properties of the crisis state. Observations from your experience which you cannot translate to the above summary should be gathered and watched. All concepts must stand the test of usefulness in practice.

II

SEVEN ESSENTIAL ATTACHMENTS

Serving those in distress creates situations every day in which we must answer questions that cast a long shadow over a person's life. What is the main trouble? What has to be accomplished? What are the most urgent tasks? How will we know when our service has reached its objective? The way in which we organize our energies to approach such decisions can have a far-reaching impact on the effectiveness of our work, and deserves corresponding attention.

Most often, the information we use to make such decisions relates to a small number of task-defining observations. *Is the machinery of the body intact or is it damaged or altered?* Issues of genetic inheritance, biochemistry, nutrition, toxins, damaged parts, altered anatomy and addiction to a narcotic material, are examples of situations in which altered bodily machinery can influence behavior. *What are this individual's characteristic patterns of behavior during stress?* What adaptive styles does he use when under challenge? Suspicion, flight, impulsiveness, caution, searching, testing and seeking assistance from other people, exemplify terms used to describe key elements of behavior during an adaptive challenge. (We shall consider problems associated with particular adaptive styles later.) *What is the individ-*

ual's prior experience with professional helpers and treat-ment-oriented activities? How frequent or persisting is his use of the patienthood role? Does he move into patienthood relationships seeking assistance, moratorium or sanctuary? How successful have various kinds of assistance been in the past? (At another time, we shall consider ways of estimating the current impact of prior treatment experiences.) Can we discover the status of an individual's essential categories of organic exchange with his environment? Are the life-sup-porting, and personality-supporting, exchanges proceeding, or are there severances in these attachments?

For purposes of discussion, we have boiled down the full array of important transactions with the environment into "seven essential attachments." We have found seven basic areas of inquiry which, in our judgment, cover the majority of behaviors and situations; this gives our clinical survey sufficient range and detail without making it cumbersome. We feel, parenthetically, that regular use of a standardized set of survey areas can be a useful tool from several points of view: there is the value that resides in a familiar format; the fact that repeated use of a decision tool like "the seven essen-tial attachments" can allow a group of people who work to-gether to develop a shared, coordinative approach. The breadth and focus inherent in a strategically designed as-sessment plan assist the helpers to avoid the hazards of fixed or narrowed styles of professional thinking. Handy practices which facilitate an organized scan can lead to more precise responses during the worrisome, often chaotic flow of events at crisis.

Each of the seven categories of necessary transaction with the environment is, considered separately, essential. Considered as a set, they are a relatively complete account of all connections. Each is necessary for a person's survival; the seven, when intact, are sufficient for survival. The categories of attachment are interdependent, or "cantilevered." If one kind of attachment remains severed for more than a brief in-terval, damage spreads to other kinds of attachments. Each type of attachment is like the need for oxygen; if the orga-nism looses its attachment to, or exchange with, oxygen, it dies. And the organism needs oxygen even if it has abundant supplies of water and food.

Here, then, are the seven essential attachments:

1. To: *Food, oxygen, and information of requisite variety: biochemical and informational supplies;*
2. To: *A clear concept of a self-identity, held with conviction;*
3. To: *Persons, at least one, in persisting, interdependent contact, occasionally approximating intimacy;*
4. To: *Groups, at least one, comprised of individuals who regard this person as a member;*
5. To: *Roles, at least one, which offer a context for achieving dignity, and self-esteem, through performance;*
6. To: *Money, or purchasing power, to participate in an exchange of goods and services in a society specialized for such exchanges;*
7. To: *A comprehensive system of meaning, a satisfying set of notions which clarify experience and define ambiguous events.*

Diagram 1 illustrates two features of the seven necessary attachments: the necessity of each, and the sufficiency of the set.

"Necessity," here, means that the person, or the personality, atrophies if any attachment is severed. "Sufficiency" means that, taken as a set, the seven attachments include all the lines of behavior known to maintain a vital exchange with the environment.

Diagram 2 characterizes the seven essential attachments in a little more detail.

ATTACHMENT #1: SUPPORTS NECESSARY TO EXISTENCE

The first attachment is to food, oxygen, and information.[5,8] This basal attachment includes material exchanges which draw in supplies for the construction of the body and

Diagram 1
THE SEVEN ESSENTIAL ATTACHMENTS

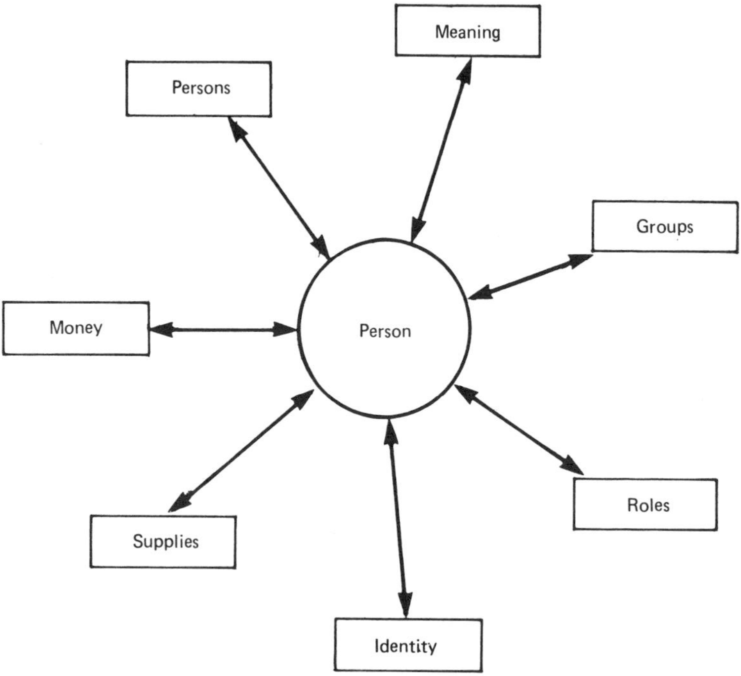

inputs of sensation which comprise the building blocks of personality. If the supplies of oxygen are interrupted, even briefly, damage or death quickly follows. When supplies of sensation and information are interrupted, the disorganization of personality starts almost as quickly, and spreads progressively. Those situations which involve an almost complete interruption of all forms of sensation are often quite dramatic, as, for example, the chemical interruption during clinical anesthesia, the anatomical interruption of spinal injuries, or the laboratory insulations of "sensory deprivation." Such interruptions of sensory intake regularly result in panic, disorganization, degrees of psychosis and marked impairment of social performance. Less dramatic, but equally hazardous, are the more prolonged, though less complete, interruptions of sensation which routinely accompany a confinement to bed, imprisonment, hospitalization, or certain solitary styles of life. Abundantly flowing raw sensation provides a necessary engine for experience. *Informative variety and pattern provide organization to the experiencer as well as body to the experience.*[4,5,8] When the flow of information is severely restricted, as in confinement to an institu-

Diagram 2
THE SEVEN ESSENTIAL ATTACHMENTS

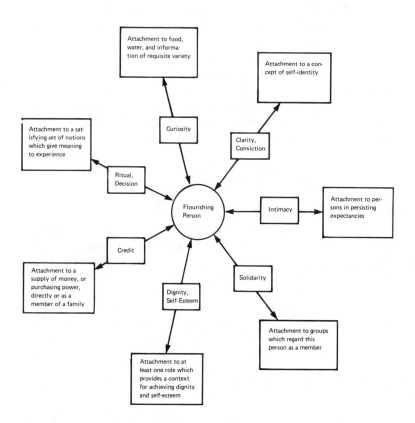

tion, or to a home for the elderly, or when an active person is confined to bed, the attachment to information often must be considered severed, or at risk of severance.

Every person normally exercises a *control of flow of information,* which must be sharply distinguished from a *severance of flow.* Individuals regularly set aside specific intervals during the day and week when they meditate, rest or sleep. During such periods there is an active, organized restriction of the intake of sensation. This "gating" of the flow of information is quite different from a sudden or progressive interruption of information. Ordinary rhythmic regulation of intake is selective and partial. It has a daily, weekly or seasonal pattern, and is easy to distinguish from the enveloping, persisting type of reduction in flow which has the functional effect of a severance.

The status of an individual's attachment to supplies of information can be monitored through observations of the presence of *curiosity.*[2] The affect, or emotional accompaniment, to the registration of sensory experience can vary from intense curiosity to disinterested apathy. The presence of curiosity, even intermittently, signals that the attachment to information is intact. The feeling tone known as curiosity not only facilitates the internal mechanics of the search-and-registry faculties, but provides a social signal that the person is in an activated state as regards his seeking, pattern-sensing and "hooking onto" new information. When an individual is attached to his flow of sensation he automatically informs his social surround, using built-in affect signals, that he is seeking and reacting to that flow. The searching, scanning and signaling qualities of the transactions with sensation illustrate the "two-way" flow intrinsic to all the attachments.[2] Observations concerning curiosity comprise a handy and reasonably reliable monitor of the status of an individual's attachment to a flow of information.

ATTACHMENT #2: THE NOTION OF IDENTITY

The second category of attachment is to a clear notion of

identity, a picture of self.[3,4] Human beings appear to organize their transient ongoing perceptions and behavior around a more enduring picture, or "map," of the self and its possibilities. A notion of the self embodying reasonably clear outlines is an essential feature of the machinery within which events are sorted. The self-identity is constantly being constructed and repaired. Some components of identity are observations an individual makes about himself. Some are observations others have offered to him. Some are decisions he has made which "fix" critical features and define "the essential self." Some are beliefs an individual holds about his probable behavior in various conceivable circumstances. Such notions of the self and its possibilities, "furnish" the future with imaginable events and constitute a type of planning, a guide for deciding.

It appears that the internally experienced picture of the self is most useful to an individual when it elicits sharp outlines and is accompanied by affects of conviction, or certitude.[3,4,5,8] A person needs to know exactly what kind of person he is, and he needs to know it with conviction. To the extent that a person loses clear notions of who he is, or loses a sense of conviction about such notions, or simultaneously experiences a range of critically different definitions of his "self," he becomes immobilized from decision. He may be said to be "dissociated." Diffusion of previously clear notions, or "fogging" of the self-image, is a salient characteristic of persons-in-distress. Such a loss of clarity is also characteristic of persons placed in situations where their usually experienced picture of the self appears incorrect or does not seem to apply. Late adolescents and young adults often do not have a clear identity when they move beyond the family circle. Persons in the early adult years have not yet fully worked out a picture of the self which "suits" them. Consequently, they frequently pass through episodes of distress which mark major events in the work of self-assembly. Older adults may lose a clear notion of identity when events remove them from a social field of people "who know them." Older persons can also lose the experience of identity when they are thrust into situations in which their existing descriptions of self seem irrelevant, apparently neither confirmed nor denied by contact with the ongoing material of current experience.

Observations centering on clarity and conviction appear to comprise the most revealing monitor of the integrity of the attachment to a self-view. The problem of assessment is to monitor the effectiveness of the self-view as a gyroscope in the flux of experience. Preoccupation with other features of the identity may sometimes distract us from this task, because such specific features are thought to be indices of mental health. For instance, "maturity," "appropriateness," and "accuracy" are examples of clinical judgments often made about the self-view. Important though such attributes of the self-picture may be, we cannot use them in assessing the integrity of the attachment to an identity, anymore than we would concentrate on the color of a yardstick we were employing to reckon distance. The gyroscopic vitality of the self-view is revealed to the observer primarily through the clarity and certitude accompanying its operations. When observers are absorbed in considering whether one particular identity is attractive to others, or whether they would like to number a person with such an identity among their friends, they are in a distinctly different field of play. The assessment of current adaptive capacity is ordinarily not assisted by considering whether an identity is interesting or laudatory. The assessment of identity as a category of attachment to a surround is strictly oriented to its impact as a guiding force in defining that individual's experience. Before one can consider the advantages of alternative routes, one must establish the integrity of the rudder and helm.

ATTACHMENT #3: CONNECTION WITH OTHER PERSONS

An individual requires a persisting attachment to at least one person.[2,3,4,9] A person attachment is recognizable when the individual is in a "personal situation" where both parties react in a manner dependent on the past and expectable future behavior of the other. The floor upon which attachments to persons are based appears to be an attitude of persisting curiosity about another person, in a field of expectable, nonsurprising thoughts about that other person. As in the case with the attachment to an identity, there is a sharp distinction between basal properties like interest and persistence, and accessory qualities like maturity, mutuality and experience-sharing. The professional assessment of the attachment-to-persons allocates central importance to the features of duration and interlocked curiosities, because the details of direct human contact activity are so widely varying in other respects. An individual needs to experience connectedness to another person before he can interest himself in secondary issues of "quality." Apparently, a continuing flow of recollected experiences of a type associated with interlocking behaviors in close space, or "private space," comprises the material for the feeling of a connectedness. The sharp distinction between basal properties of the attachment, like persistence and interactivity, from accessory qualities, like benevolence and nurturance, has an importance which can be illustrated by glancing at their playout in treatment decisions. For instance, clinicians would not act to separate a person from a primary human relationship because they observed it to be full of fighting, any more than they would shut off a supply of oxygen because of an accompanying bad odor. Professional assistance with rebuilding and improving relationships may avoid the severance of basal attachments. "Therapeutic" severance of primary relationships is seldom helpful, because it may force an individual to attach to treatment staff as the only remaining anchor-to-persons. Professional helping styles which encourage the severance of "toxic" primary relationships lead to unnecessary recruitment into disability states, and are closely linked with sanctuarial patterns of service.

One can assess the status of an individual's basal attachment to persons by noting whether he arranges for repeating contacts. For instance, it is often useful to ask about the events of a recent week. Persons regularly mentioned in such reports comprise attachment figures. When an individual can report no repeating meetings or "presences" with another, there is no person attachment. Ordinarily, an individual cannot, with dignity, directly report the absence of friendships. Most often, he signals the severance of the person attachment by offering descriptions of his solitary status in the recollected events he offers. The report of even a small number of events of intimacy, of private, unique communication in close space, can reveal the presence of a basal attachment to persons. Frequent mental images of another person, perhaps together with eye or skin contact with that person, or behavior directed toward the maintenance of interlocking activity with that person, signal us the attachment to persons is operative.

ATTACHMENT #4: CONNECTION TO GROUPS

An individual needs an attachment to at least one group fully as much as to oxygen or persons.[2,3,5,6] The presence of an attachment to a group is revealed by any repeating activity with a cluster of persons who regard the individual as a member. Usually the individual regards himself as a member. Basal attachment groups can include, for example, work groups, religious groups, social groups or political groups. The dominant grouping for many persons is one based on a family, one related by kinship. But the central feature of such primary groups, as basal attachments, is a capacity to generate the affect of solidarity. All persons require at least one group attachment which can assist in ongoing tasks like provision of food, shelter and recreation, and which can also assist in managing episodes of unusual challenge. And an individual signals, using exchanges of sentiments of solidarity, which groups comprise his primary interest as attachment objects. Solidarity-linked conduct is a signaling system which has the effect of letting the members of a regularly clustering set of persons know of the group-oriented interest of others in the set. It is a multilateral marker of readiness for continuing attachment. The existence of this group-directed signaling activity provides a handy marker that an individual has available a group attachment. If he can report regular activity in specific settings, with clusters of persons, accompanied by sentiments of solidarity, he is attached.

All people experience an active curiosity about each others' attachments. For instance, human beings continuingly show interest in the signals offered to them about the attachments in use by those in their ambience. They show a keen attention to the patterns of flow of curiosity in their associates (attachment to information), and to conduct in which their associates take pride (identity). People are vigilant for cues which disclose intimacy events (attachments to persons), and solidarity signals (attachments to groups). The principal difference between such attachment-monitoring activity as conducted in ordinary life and such activity as associated with professional caregiving lies in the questions under surveillance. In everyday life people are seeking to know *which* objects in their field may be providing attachments for associates. In clinical work, professionals are interested in knowing *whether* an individual is attached at all. The reader can easily follow, in his own experience, the differences between an inquiry about *whether* there is attachment versus one about to *what*.

ATTACHMENT #5: CONNECTION TO A SOCIAL ROLE

Each person needs to have the opportunity to perform in congruence with at least one persisting social role.[3,4,5,6,9] Intrinsic to that role must be conduct that is assessable by the public. Whether milkman, teacher, mother, child, steelworker, friend or clown, each person needs to have skills, and settings, to show that he "can do." And not just that he can do in general, but in particular. A person needs to be able to show he can accomplish a task. He needs to show he can attract people and interest others in helping him. He needs to demonstrate he can serve a useful purpose to others. From such observations as he and others make about his performance, according to publicly shared standards of excellence, he can come to regard himself with esteem. And others, assessing his performance according to the requirements of roles and situations, can confer value and dignity on his public presence. The vital functions which dignity and self-esteem play are illustrated in situations where they may be absent—in persons in prisons and institutions, in persons applying for unemployment income benefits, and in persons within a state of acute panic. Self-esteem breathes oxygen into the painful, uncharted journey of meeting an adaptational challenge. Self-esteem creates a signaling field which draws others from the social surround into efforts to assist in a situation. Dignity originates in the surrounding field and carries to a person a promissory offer of assistance, or dutiful conduct by the field, should the need arise. Dignity transactions, as offered in ordinary situations, are a signaling "paint" applied to portions of the interlocking conduct between a person and members of his social field. Such signals include posture, dress, greetings, solicitous manner and other conventions. In situations of distress, dignity transactions carry an additional possibility, one which can "command" a dutiful, non-supplicant call for assistance. The impact of dignity transactions is also illustrated in situations where dignity is absent or even "negative." For example, the condition of "stigma" or untouchability may be regarded as dignity with a negative valence. If the valence is "positive," the field is signaled to approach the signaler; because the valence is "negative," the field is signaled to distance itself from the signaler.

The contribution of self-esteem and dignity to the continuing work of adaptation and survival highlight the fact that esteem on the part of surrounding people and groups is a necessary component of such work. We shall have more to say about the relationship of the "corporate substrate" to certain adaptive endeavors at a later point. Linkage to a persisting social role, with availability of skills and opportunities for its performance, are so necessary to survival that we must ascertain that such linkage in fact exists. Any situation that confines an individual to an institution, or that drastically constricts one's social or physical action-in-the-world, frequently presents the hazard of severing role attachments.

Any situation that holds no opportunity for excellence of role conduct, save in the role of patient, or casualty, will sever the attachment-to-role. Migration, social upheaval or personal injury can similarly break vital role linkages to the social environment.

The process of aging regularly causes a change in role-attachments which should be considered separately. Aging generally changes the ground rules for acquiring self-esteem and dignity. Early in the life-cycle, competent performance, publicly assessed, creates the linkage to self-esteem and dignity. By the time a person moves into the later years, some free-floating self-esteem and dignity have ordinarily been acquired. Because an aged person has a "reputation," an individual and his field can transact attitudes of dignity and self-esteem on the basis of recollections of past conduct. The situation is less dependent on current, daily displays. The evolution of "free-floating" dignity and self-esteem somewhat alters the later dynamics of the sick role. But even in later years, there remains a central requirement either to display or to recollect a set of observations which can form a basis for conferring dignity and self-esteem.

ATTACHMENT #6: MONEY AND PURCHASING POWER

Most human beings interact with one or another organized national system of trade and economic exchange. Such economic participation greatly increases people's material standard of living—food, shelter, clothing, goods and services. It expands their options and security far beyond that which could be created by their individual, solitary labor. But the amplification of human energies made possible by such economic exchange is only available to persons who achieve a linkage, through cash purchasing power, to the economic system. The situation of an individual without purchasing power is similar to that of a primitive hunter and gatherer, one without the skills for such work.[9] Cash is the vehicle of attachment to the communal engine. The absence

of cash unhooks an individual from most communal benefits, except for a few rights which derive from citizenship or
residence in a particular locale. The term "poverty," denoting
the condition of non-linkage to the economic engine, has
come to connote a more general injury. The term is used to
summarize a set of general miseries-of-condition—including
grave gaps in access to effective health and educational services—that result from economic unlinkage. The unlinked
condition is commonly regarded as the cause, and result, of a
progressive disability. Also, parents that are separated from
economic linkages transmit, more often than not, the same
life-style to their children; a pattern of personal development
that does not equip the child to link himself to the engine
later in life.

Because "non-attachment" to the economy results in a
disturbance to human behavior that is profound and progressive, the helper must discover the condition of the economic attachment. The ability to maintain this linkage has a
vital significance similar to the significance of the other connections. Services that intend to be helpful, but neglect to
enhance this attachment, often produce evanescent results.
This fact is background to the disappointing results of services to persons who are socially isolated, migrant, aged or
resident in households without a breadwinner. Whatever
specific help a narrow "sectoral" service might offer, if it does
not repair the linkage to the economy, its benefit may fade
before larger forces.

Linkage to the economy is ordinarily effected through
holding a job, or through income property, or via membership in a family unit containing a jobholder or property hold-
er. Although there are many variations to the mechanics of
remaining connected to the economic engine, those which
yield cash, rather than provisions, are most flexible. It is
usually possible, for example, to assess the integrity of the
economic linkage by considering a person's clothing or shelter. Or it can be discovered by considering a person's weekly
activities and daily schedule. Employment, purchasing power, or a family-linked call on such power, reveal themselves

easily in the fabric of a week's activities. If the integrity of the linkage is still in doubt, the observer can ask himself whether he would lend this person a thousand dollars. If he would worry about the individual's capacity to repay, he has likely answered his question. Members of some rural families, and residents of some institutions, possess very little cash or direct purchasing power, and yet are not always unlinked. Although they may both demonstrate reduced social excursion, and reduced variety of activities, they remain attached.

ATTACHMENT #7: A SYSTEM OF MEANING

The seventh attachment is to a personally experienced, comprehensive system of meaning. Each person carries a residue of notions, some in words, some in images, which guide his decisions in the conduct of affairs.[1,5,8,9] It is possible to think of this system of orienting experiences as a general purpose "map" for movement through life. The creation and use of such a map are continuously active tasks. These tasks appear to maintain a call on the everyday flow of attention from childhood through old age. Guiding observations, when put into words, are discussed under terminologies variously called "religious," "ethical," "life-style" or "common-sense." Several kinds of emotion signal the exercise of such orienting notions. The feelings associated with "offense," or "properness," or "meaningfulness" are examples. Any person in a state of attachment to his comprehensive system of meaning has a regular flow of experiences which suggest to him what is important, proper, conventional, or, conversely, what is wrong, outside of duty, or outside his style-of-life.

In assessing whether an individual is in contact with his comprehensive system of meaning, the observer looks for options in the individual's current crisis which the person regards either as forbidden or required. Or he may perceive them as connected with a deep sense of "self-expression." When particular options for action are clothed with abundant feeling or with a sense of urgency, they are linked with the meaning system. If an individual respects some of his options for action by investing them with careful planning, we can know he is connected with his system of meaning.

Let us sharply distinguish efforts to figure out *whether* an individual is in contact with a system of meaning, from an inquiry into the *content* of any such meaning. Assessment of the integrity of the attachment is the task. Loss of the attachment can lead to profound impairments of adaptive capacity, and therefore this loss is of concern to the observer; whereas assessment of the content of an individual's system of meaning is seldom a legitimate concern of helpers. (Later, as part of some specific service designs, we will describe activities which aim to communicate parts of the meaning system in words. Such activities can often make the value system more of an active factor in carrying out current adaptational tasks, and thus provide a significant clinical approach.)

Several other phenomena can help the observer ascertain the existence of connections to a system of meaning. The presence of ritual activity, or celebration, or reaffirmation of core value notions, suggest that an individual is linked effectively. Human beings spend a significant fraction of their time keeping a core value system "alive" so that it may be available when called into decision-making activity during episodes of challenge.

In crisis, many persons show a peculiar relationship to their sense of meaning. They show a special state of consciousness in which many possible meanings, or options, or attitudes flow before their attention in a kaleidoscope of briefly held "moments of conviction." Most often this situation suggests that an attachment is partially severed, but not lost. In clinical states of depression, as well as in several other situations which "freeze" the adaptive machinery, many individuals report an experience wherein *all* options seem forbidden or undesirable. In such situations, the map of meaning is still present, but in an inverse form. It appears as a "laundry list of complaints" or as a round-and-round rumination about "impossibilities." In both of these situations, the attachment to the system of meaning, although partly severed, usually may be repaired through the action of others. We will examine later what actions others may take to repair the linkage to a system of meaning.

Linkage to the comprehensive system of meaning is vital to the continuance of personality and the work of adaptation. As the system of meaning interacts with the ongoing flow of experience, it generates a personal experience of position, direction and course. This interaction provides a calculus for reckoning *what* is going on, what *action* should be taken and *why* such action is worthy. Throughout life, but especially at time of crisis, an individual needs to have such an operating calculus. For the work of adaptation, an individual needs a way to reckon the "right" status of the world around him and his correct relation to it. He needs to be able to discover his proper activities in the course of events, and to ascertain his likely pathways to joy. Efforts to energize the use of this guidance system are one of the principle activities of helpers.

SUMMARY

Perspectives which describe the ordinary social attachments of human beings can give direction to our efforts to assist distressed persons conduct their work of adaptation. The concept of "seven essential attachments" is such a perspective. It is designed to direct the attention of helpers toward "the larger picture," as they assess a troubled individual's current situation. Out of such a view, we may come to know the forces we are working to draw into harness. Table 2 reviews the definitions and major findings which may assist in assessing the integrity of each of the attachments.

Table 2

A FRAMEWORK FOR ASSESSING THE INTEGRITY OF SEVEN ESSENTIAL ATTACHMENTS

Category of Attachment	Observation, or Type of Affect, Used to Monitor Integrity of Attachment	Usual Maintenance Operations for Attachment	Setting or Experience Which Places Strain on Attachment
1. To: Supplies of food, oxygen and information of requisite variety	Presence of curiosity	Searching, scanning, using, altering input	Institutions, isolation, poverty, health crises
3. To: Persons (with opportunity for persisting, repeating contacts)	Intimacy, even occasionally; tenderness, concern; (do not disqualify because of other, non-tender affects)	Close space, language, touching; prolonged or repeating, shared experience or activities	Living alone, institutions, migration, deaths, health losses
2. To: Identity (notions describing the self to the self)	Clarity of self-view; conviction or sense of belief concerning accuracy of particular options for self-expression	Weighing options for attractiveness or congruence with self-view (ruling in and ruling out)	Crisis-in-transit experience, failures (acute or chronic); placement in a setting that has no knowledge of a person's identity, aspirations, past experience

4.	To: Groups (work, play, social, religious, domiciliary, kin and clan)	Solidarity (person and group both report solidarity)	Living alone, institutions, migration, performance crises
5.	To: Roles (persisting, repeating, public, observable behavior)	Presence of skills and opportunities to perform roles; Self-esteem, dignity	Institutionalization, unemployment, migration, chronic poverty status, old age, health impairment, social upheaval
6.	To: The cash economy (for any culture organized around a cash market)	Would you lend this person $1000? Purchasing power for basics plus security cushion	Poverty, living alone, old age, migration, loss of family unit by death or migration
7.	To: A comprehensive system of meaning (life-style, religious, ethical)	Presence of ritual activity or notions of forbidden or imperative options in current predicament	Regular rituals keeping, or cherishing, some notions of "the good life," or which activate personal precepts defining or identifying desirable options	Crisis-in-transit experience, performance failures, isolation, placement in unfamiliar settings, loss of usual corporate surround

III

ELEMENTARY MECHANICS
OF ADAPTIVE WORK

As the waters rise, some complain, some pray,
and some build an ark.
Paraphrased from *Genesis,* Chapters 5-9

At the center of life is the necessity for surviving changing circumstances, for modifying prior ways of living. At the
center of adaptive work is a basic set of biosocial mechanics
for discovering and altering that portion of patterned behavior which has been maintained until its moment of challenge
by the flow of events. It is often our clinical aim to provide a
type of help that is grounded in activities that are intrinsic to
these problem-solving processes of adaptation. A picture of
the regular steps in adaptive work offers a convenient background for organizing such clinical activities. In the journey
we will make through the territory of human adaptational
behavior, we will focus our attention on a small class of strategic observations. Those events which appear to be regular
and necessary will call for special attention. We shall take a
particularly close look, because it is centrally important in
clinical assessments, at the emotional signaling language
which a person uses to keep the social surround—which
sometimes becomes vitally interested—abreast of the devel-

opment of adaptive efforts. The decision to highlight the social and signaling mechanics of adaptation is nourished by several premises offered earlier (See Chapter I).

Guideline 8:   The necessity for input by the social surround, in order to release the adaptive potential of crisis, is the radical center of designs for service, professional and folk. Provision for participation with a social surround during the conduct of adaptive work is a necessary (but not sufficient) component of much helping activity.

Guideline 9:   A necessary (but not sufficient) condition for establishing the care-giving relationship is the approximation, within a close, signaling exchange, of a person-in-crisis and one or more persons *not* in crisis.

Guideline 6—*restated:*   Growth-promoting types of care-giving activity avoid a focus on chemical or sanctuarial approaches to the relief of distress, when possible, and aim to facilitate the work of decision and action. The emergence of adaptive behavior offers the most desirable and least recruitatory resolution of a challenge.

As an introduction to a terminology for discussing several of the regularities at any adaptive challenge, let us consider the story of "Noah and the Ark." In the chart that follows, the phrases taken from the story of Noah comprise an arbitrary selection, in sequence, of an oral tradition that finds expression in the lore of many peoples in many places * Because the story of Noah's management of a

* "Noah and the Ark" is told in Genesis, Chapters 5-9. The story of "Prometheus and the Chest," wherein Prometheus manages his family's affairs so that they might survive a deluge comes from the Greek oral tradition. (See, for instance, Edith Hamilton, Mythology, Boston,

challenge has been processed by so many tellings, it may represent an accounting in "folk journalism" of structural regularities the tellers have recognized in any successful management of a threat to survival. (See chart pages 54-56.)

The story of Noah offers an accounting, in folk journalism, of the steps in an episode of adaptive work. It illustrates that there is a "before," "during," and "after," and a recognizable sequence within "during." The general nature of the task during any adaptive challenge is to preserve survival by innovating a set of activities which carry that which is essential through a hazardous circumstance, into a pattern of circumstances more congenial to survival. The behavioral regulation of homeostasis[1-3], or the management of a threat to survival, may result from random activities elicited in a distress period, but is more likely to result from a new pattern of behavior adapted to the situation. Generally speaking, cognition, decision, action and assessment are present, and are intrinsic to the activities of an adaptive interval. The story of Noah tells of a situation in which a threat was managed by novel, purposeful action. If we assume the term "god" stands for various social surrounds, Noah made decisions and took actions growing out of assessments and plans he constructed in collaboration with such a social surround.

Before we further outline the mechanics of the problem-solving process, let us compare problem solving with several other vital, but more automatic adaptive adjustments. Man is aided in his efforts to survive challenge by an array of adaptational subsystems: biochemical, physiologic, perceptual-cognitive-behavioral and social. The biochemical and physiologic mechanisms for meeting changing circumstances are largely informed through genetic instructions. They do not involve a large element of learning. Many of their operations bypass conscious awareness entirely. Their

---

Little, Brown and Co., 1940, Chapter 4.) There are similar stories, such as the Hindu "Manu and the Ark," "The Epic of Gilgamesh" from Mesopotamia, as well as many others (including American Indian versions), which offer startlingly similar elements.

SCHEMATIZATION OF THE STORY OF NOAH

Noah's Story	More General Account	Central Task, Activity and Signaling at Each Step
1. And Noah was five hundred years old and begat Shem, Ham, and Japheth (5:32).†	1. There was a man who had acquired a measure of habits and ways of life.	1. Steady-state. Calm before the storm.
2. And the Lord said I will destroy man, and beast, and the creeping things from the face of the Earth (6:7).	2. A profound threat came to his whole existence and manner of life.	2. Environmental change. Problem. Challenge.
3. And God said to Noah, the end of all flesh is before me (6:13).	3. He recognized that a danger was imminent.	3. Alarm, urgency. *Distress, anguish.* Detect a dangerous situation.
4. Make thee an ark (6:14).	4. He decided to take a specific action, one likely to meet the danger well.	4. Organizing a response. Search, decide, act. *Curiosity, vigilance.* Face the danger.
5. The length of the ark shall be three hundred cubits (6:15). Seal it with pitch in and out (6:14).	5. He considered several options and selected a type of action offering likely promise of success.	5. Thinking it through. *Perplexity, suspicion.* Move directively.
6. And though I do bring a flood of waters upon the earth, and everything that is in the earth shall die, with thee I establish My covenant and thou shalt come into the ark (6:17-18).	6. He acquired resolve concerning his plan. Mindful of the hazard of inaction, and aware he could not have secure knowledge, in advance, of success, he decided to place his best plan into action.	6. Seeing it through. *Hope, faith, resolve.* Make it happen.

† References are to *Genesis*, King James Version, by chapter and verse.

Noah's Story	More General Account	Central Task, Activity and Signaling at Each Step
7. Take of every beast, male and female, two by two, into the ark (6:19).	7. He made provision that his plan would carry that which was significant and valued from his past way of life into his future.	7. Rebuilding what is beloved. *Reminiscence, self-esteem.* Maintain your valuables.
8. And it rained for seven days (7:4) and the rain was upon the earth forty days and forty nights (7:12). And God made a wind to pass over the earth (8:1) and the waters returned from off the earth (8:3).	8. The threatening situation came upon him rapidly, evolving over several days. The crisis-in-transit period lasted a matter of several weeks, during which he was out of touch with his earlier state of affairs but not yet successfully arranged into his new circumstances.	8. Experiencing an interval of chaos. *Panic, patience.* The interval of chaos intrinsic to the process of change is turbulent but finite. The storm and the clearing.
9. And the ark rested on Mount Ararat (8:4). He sent forth a dove to see if the waters were abated (8:8).	9. His plan seemed to be working out satisfactorily. He took pains to check out the result of his plan.	9. Looking for the result of the action. *Testing, detecting* outcome. The plan may or may not have managed the problem.
10. But the dove found no rest and returned into the ark (8:9).	10. The danger needed more management, was not fully handled as yet.	10. Outcome monitoring. *Caution, control.* Control any impulses to perceive success when it is not present.

Noah's Story	More General Account	Central Task, Activity and Signaling at Each Step
11. After another seven days a dove returned, and in her mouth was an olive leaf (8:11) and after another seven days he sent for the dove which returned not unto him anymore (8:12).	11. He was becoming increasingly sure he had effectively managed the challenge.	11. Knowing what you are looking for. *Confidence.* Keep your eye on the ball.
12. And Noah went forth, and his sons, and his wife, and his sons' wives with him (8:18).	12. Having decided the challenge was over and mastered, he went back to the events of a more regular life.	12. Starting life again. *Relaxing, rejoicing.* When it's over, it's over.
13. And God said, I will remember my covenant which is between me and you and the waters shall no more become a flood to destroy all flesh (9:15).	13. Having come through a period of hazard successfully he was stronger and more resourceful for the experience.	13. Taking stock of what has happened. *Learning.* Moving ahead.
14. And Noah planted a vineyard (9:20) and lived after the flood three hundred and fifty years (9:28). And the days of Noah were nine hundred and fifty years: and he died (9:29).	14. He had many rather more ordinary days after the challenge.	14. Successful handling of an adaptive challenge can lead to continued survival and flourishing.

automatic activities offer dependability at a cost of flexibility.

Consider, for example, several cases of adaptive challenge which might involve changes in room temperature. If a room is getting "too warm," an individual may first start to sweat. The sweating response, which may quite effectively maintain the proper body temperature, is an example of a response selected and started automatically. It can completely bypass consciousness, and uses body systems substantially patterned by chromosomally-transmitted inheritance. Heat-induced sweating also exemplifies a situation in which the type of response and amount of response are controlled by sensory detectors which do not require learned perceptual discriminations. There are no necessary decisions concerning what is occuring.

However, let us say the temperature rises a little higher. The individual may remove a sweater or open a window. Such regulatory activity is also thermostatic, or homeostatic, or "adaptive," but it includes a mixture of learned and automatic systems. The occasion (discomfort) of a need to make an adaptive response, and the type of problem (too hot), are identified by genetically transmitted systems (thermosensors). But the behavioral response (opening the window) involves some learning from prior experience, as well as a measure of decision, action, and assessment. In such a situation, the adaptive response involves a brief use of the inventory-appraisal-decision-action-review sequence, a pattern which is at the heart of all human problem-solving activity.

Take the situation a step further into the domain of nonautomatic adaptational work. Suppose the individual experiences even more rise in temperature, and detects the sounds and smells of fire. He may leave the room or sound a warning to others, and conduct other rescue or social signaling activities. Such activities involve elements of figuring out what is happening, considering possibilities for action, deciding, doing and assessing effects. Whether the type of challenge is large or small, slow or fast in onset, whether easy (automatic) or calling for innovation, a similar set of adaptive steps can be observed:

1. *Discovery of the presence of a challenge event; discomfort;* something is lost, changed, hurting, different; dazed search for bearings; anguished call of distress;

2. *Recognizing the nature of the challenging event; perplexity;* search, inventory, quandary, reminiscence;

3. *Constructing and considering several possibilities for action; suspicion; vigilance;* figuring out the best path to carry the most of what is valued into the most attractive future;

4. *Deciding: selecting the best possibility for action; complaining, plaintive;* comparing the options for feasibility in the situation, compatibility with attractive futures and cross-testing ideas with persons in the surround;

5. *Taking action according to the selected plan; hope, faith, resolve;* seeing it through, enduring, struggling, "hanging-in;"

6. *Evaluation of results: OK?; not OK?;* outcome monitoring, waiting, checking, testing, recycling the problem- solving sequence when necessary;

7. *Return to ordinary state:* celebration, relaxation, taking pride.

These seven steps are visible in Noah's story, in the handling of the fire, and in many situations of challenge, distress and response. Each of the steps is essential, even though any single step may (or may not) last a very short time. Each step must occur in sequence. Each step depends upon what has occurred before. Each step is carried on in a context of specific emotions, or affects, which biologically facilitate the activities of that step, and which signal the social surround concerning the phase and pace of the adaptational work in process. The successful accomplishment of each step is effected, sometimes critically so, by concurrent transactions with a social surround. "Helping" is a term referring to such transactions between the individual and his surround. And helping moves through a matching set of seven steps.

An opening glimpse at adaptational work is offered by studies of human beings dealing with particular kinds of challenge. Particularly helpful are studies that deal with infants separating from the mother[4,5], handling the death of a loved one[6], facing severe illness[7], dealing with choice points in the life cycle[8], and studies considering the behavior of human groups in environmental disasters[9-11]. Although descriptions of patterns of human behavior during adaptive episodes are primitive and exploratory, it is already possible to discover striking regularities across diverse types of challenges. Several of these regularities in problem-solving work appear to display the beginnings of useful guidelines for individuals attempting to renew the momentum of adaptive work when it has gone awry.

STEP ONE: DISCOVERY OF THE PRESENCE OF A CHALLENGE EVENT

Precept: The problem-solving process does not commence until the individual decides he has perceived a clear and undeniable hazard or loss.

Affect-Signals: Anxiety, panic, terror, dread, daze, pain, anger, shock, call of distress, cry.

The organism apparently does not move into the adaptational sequence for trivial reasons. The sequence calls for abrupt changes in patterns of behavior and heavy expenditures of energy. There are risks of death and injury which follow from the reduced behavioral precision during the "disorganized" middle phases of the adaptive sequence. Individuals remember the pain and terror of the middle phases, and ordinarily express little appetite for more. When the infant is removed from the mother, there is a lag-time before intense protest-crying commences[4]. In disasters of flood and tornado there is a delay, sometimes with lethal consequences, in deciding that the cues of a hazard must be taken seriously[9/10]. Following death of a beloved person, the survivors regularly appear to entertain many delaying or circumventing formulations to explain their recent perceptions before deciding that a tragic event is upon them[6]. In the case of the onset of a massive disability, such as the paralysis of poliomyelitis, individuals appear to "face the problem" gradually, in a stepped series of expanding awarenesses[7]. They appear to be "gating" the intake of information with an eye on their capacity to maintain a basal level of organization. They are actively regulating the pace of onset into the adaptational sequence. Activities which regulate the pace of gaining a cognitive grasp of the situation, so that it may come neither too slowly (denial) or too quickly (panic), appear intrinsic to successful adaptive work[12]. Such regulation results from an automatic interplay between the challenged individual and his surround[6-9,12]. The signaling affects associated with the "onset phase" (dread, pain, daze) have an internal influence on starting up the search to discover what is happening[13/14]. The same affects appear to elicit automatic activities in the surround. There is prodding and inquiry which has the effect of organizing and regulating the discovery process[18,13/14]. Social surrounds move in to urge an individual "to face" a difficulty when he is reluctant to do so, or to prevent him from "running off half-cocked" when he does not appear to be properly regulating the onset of the adaptive process. The regulatory function of the social surround, which begins in step one, proceeds throughout the whole work of the adaptive sequence[7].

STEP TWO: RECOGNIZING THE NATURE OF THE CHALLENGE EVENT

Precept: No person can relinquish what he cannot identify. No person can arrange himself to deal with what he cannot detect.

Affect-Signals: Sadness, perplexity, reminiscence, protest, anger, wonder, suppliance, yearning.

The tasks of the second phase center on figuring out what the nature of the problem is and on gaining assistance in dealing with the situation. The special modes of perception and cognition that emerge during the adaptational state (see Chapter I) appear uniquely suited to the tasks of recognizing the nature of an altered circumstance, and offering behavior that is shaped appropriately. The scanning activity of attention seeks to define what is altered or missing. Role behavior "opens" to the possibility of major changes in patterning. Affectional attachments to persons, groups and projects open and reach for possibly extensive realignments. The "random access" mode of memory recall replaces the more usual, highly filtered pattern of recall. A flexible access to the registry of prior experience interplays with the scan of the current predicament. The special behavioral sequence, search-appraisal-decision-action-review, starts automatically whenever the usual calculus of reckoning is disturbed. But it does not start unless the usual calculus of reckoning is *unable* to remain undisturbed; i.e., unless the person is unable to explain what is happening.

The task of defining the current predicament requires, first, discovery of what is lost or changed, and then placement of this discovery against a background of that which remains relatively undisturbed. These reconnoitering tasks make heavy calls on the processes of perception (figure and ground) and cognition (new concept formation). In perceiving the outline of a figure on a background, the individual first detects an "edge" then a "shape" then "movement as a unit on a field." In constructing an idea, the individual uses "cues" to establish "dimensions" which can be clustered into patterns, or "objects," against the background whir and blur of experience. Adaptational work involves a step of identifying a "problem" and placing it in a context of "things that are OK." An individual who has lost a spouse frequently enters the work of bereavement by beginning to reminisce about the lost beloved[5/6]. Reminiscence is an activity which draws together many memories and current perceptions and defines the nature of a loss against a background of what remains.

The affect termed "sadness" appears to activate the reminiscence process and to signal the surround of the fact that bereavement work is underway. The person who has lost a beloved reminisces about "what we used to do together" and "what he (or she) was like"[6]. The infant looks around, listens and reaches out for the missing mother[4/5]. Persons entering college reminisce about "missing home" and "old neighborhoods" as a preface to reconnoitering current challenges like "greater autonomy"[15/16]. Persons faced with the onset of major muscular paralysis offer detailed accountings of activities "I used to do" and of situations "I will miss"[7]. Persons who have lost their vision go through an early phase of recounting lost activities like "reading the paper" and "walking (while navigating by vision) along the street"[17]. People in the surround seem to recognize that the reminiscence is an aspect of defining what must be relinquished or replaced. They take action to push the individual to "work on the problem" or "get on with life" or "count your blessings." The signaling affects of this phase are sadness, yearning, perplexity, protest, wonder and suppliance. Such affects seem to draw others from the surround into "pushing" an individual to figure out what is gone, or "what's happening," and what remains, or "putting the pieces together." The social surround also appears to assist in regulating the flow, or "gating," of reminiscence activity. If it goes too slowly, too long, or repetitiously, friends, will push it, saying, "the good old days are gone."

STEP THREE: CONSTRUCTING AND CONSIDERING SEVERAL POSSIBILITIES FOR ACTION

Precept: Group connectedness, with dignity and self-esteem, is intrinsic to opening up the possibilities for major change.

Affect-Signals: Suspicion, perplexity, doubt, complaining, anomie, helplessness, suppliance, distress.

No person can organize to carry through a response he

does not understand. The adaptational work of figuring out "what to do" carries that anguished uncertainty intrinsic to any earnest examination of possible paths for action, each an "unknown." There is a stretching, "thinking up" possibilities for action. As in the story of Noah, several possibilities usually must be considered, because seldom does the first idea appear feasible and attractive. The ability to hold several ideas, or several parts of responses, together in view at the same time is intrinsic to the task of comparison, but also an inherently destabilizing experience. Individuals seldom enjoy the instability and concentrated effort which is part of "probing" untested possibilities. They may attempt "escape" by finding fault with every possibility, or they may leap into impulsive activity which bypasses the effort of decision. The destabilizing impact which accompanies an earnest probing of several quite different paths for action, a feeling of "coming unglued," is greatly tempered by the regulatory effect of contact with other persons. A person can "open himself" to feel different possibilities when people around him ask questions like "how is it going?" and "what do you think about this?" As the individual lets it be known he is moving through that time "after what went before" but "before what I will do next," those around him move in with their more organized reactions to the situation. Persons in contact with a pool of associates during the inventory of possibilities seem to consider a wider range of options and to probe them more thoroughly[7,15,16]. The social surround appears to make a convenant with the person in distress to react to the possibilities he raises, and to let him know if he "gets too far off base." Friends of persons newly facing blindness raise and offer reactions to many possibilities. Their input to the pool of options would include learning Braille, using a guidedog, and visiting a faith-healer[17]. Associates of freshly arriving college students automatically offer reactions to "too many calls to home" and "not bothering to learn the catalog of courses"[16]. People around individuals facing the problems of major paralysis from poliomyelitis divert them from consideration of suicide and from "skipping the exercises"[7], and offer focused reactions to tasks like "managing the equipment" and "learning to use the brace"[7]. The patients who spent time in association with a group of individuals, most of whom were working on such problems, coped with their situation better and more quickly than those who stayed apart from the group[7].

The affect-signals of the adaptational phase when options are being considered include the provocative displays of persons "figuring out something." They display suspicion because they are vigilant to detect cues which would clarify events and possibilities. They display perplexity because they are suspending premature decisions about the best course. They display doubt because insufficient sorting has occurred to warrant certitude. They offer many complaints because none of the options being considered meets all criteria of attractiveness. They show anomie because they are "in between" the old ways and the yet-to-be-decided new ways. They display a category of signals sometimes called "helplessness," because such signals draw in the social surround to perform its intrinsic regulative activities during the unstable "middle part" of an adaptational episode. They are suppliant because the suppliant display orients the social field, when drawn in, toward the special activities which comprise helping. The suppliant display increases in the social field the dominance of regulatory activity over other, competing possible activities, such as eating, sleeping and resting.

Professional supports to the adaptive work of individuals in distress can use such affect-displays to detect when such work is underway and which stage is active. When professional designs for service recognize the regulatory and monitoring functions of such affect-displays, efforts to "relieve them" or medicate them fade before measures to provide a social context responsive to them.

STEP FOUR: DECIDING: SELECTING THE BEST POSSIBILITY FOR ACTION

Precept: No possibility is worthy of action which does not appear linked with an attractive future.

Affects-Signals: Conviction, certitude, impulsiveness, commandeering, demanding, discovery-aha, girding.

The activities which comprise the task of deciding are those of *picturing* what features would be embodied in a satisfactory solution, and *recognizing* that option which best displays such features. In the story of Noah, the problem-solver made sure his solution would carry the main measure of that which he valued of his past way of life (his wife and sons and two of every living thing), and make possible an attractive future. As individuals move toward the making of a decision to take an action, they appear to summon their orienting life values. "Who am I?" "What do I want to do or be?" "What is important in my life?" Individuals around an individual making an important decision seem to remind him of life goals he has earlier pursued. They recollect notions of values and life-style that might be applicable. Young adults entering college rehearse different possibilities "to see how they would fit (with values and objectives)"[16]. Couples learning to deal with the crisis of the birth of a premature infant decide their new pattern of elaborate, extra care to the infant must be "only temporary" and soon yield to "more normal" patterns[12]. After the intensely felt loss of her husband, the bereaved widow decides to return to her profession of "being a secretary, and review my French," because the path offers possibilities "for a good rebuilding"[6]. Ruminative, protracted indecision often yields to the push of a social surround which asks "where do you want to be in ten years?" The tasks of holding several options in view and recognizing the one best option lie at the heart of successful adaptational work. Much of the affect-signaling which accompanies the work of adaptation may have acquired its survival value out of the effect it has on converting the chaotic cognition of the individual-in-distress into a reliable faculty for deciding. For example, when an individual displays a large number of possible interpretations of events, along with persisting perplexity ("I don't understand"), the social surround automatically tries to push the individual to choose one of the interpretations ("Can't you see what's going on here?"). When a person seems to be cycling in a sequence of complaints, a long, whining, laundry list of complaints, the social field tries to push him to describe "how things really should be." The field tries to convert the cycling view of "how things shouldn't be" to its inverse, a picture of a valuable set of goals. Whereas the cycling series of complaints seldom seems to move toward a decision, a picture of a valuable, attractive set of goals regularly activates the making of a decision. When an individual-in-distress is displaying anger toward many people, or toward a wide range of aspects of his situation, the social field regularly says "what are you going to do about it?" In these situations of cycling perplexity, cycling complaining, cycling anger, the social field appears to act as if it is automatically signaled when to act and how to act. In each case the social surround seems to know how to act in concert to create a field with a "pressure to choose." Perplexity seems to convey to the field a signal to press for the "one best" description of what is happening. Complaining seems to start a social push to define the "one best" desired outcome. Diffuse, cycling anger seems to elicit a social push to select and take an action which will "fix" the offensive situation.

The interplay between a person-in-distress and his surround social field underlines three features of the "corporate substrate," or social input to individual adaptive work:

1. It is regulated by an unlearned set of signaling displays; i.e., dread, perplexity, suspicion, complaining, anger, etc., which automatically converts a person-plus-surround into a temporary task-oriented cluster.

2. In order for this temporary task-oriented cluster to "work," it seems to require occasional face-to-face contact within a "close signaling space."

3. The temporary task-oriented cluster can be comprised of members of an individual's regular network, for example, his family, of strangers drawn in by the distress signals, of professionals drawn in by role and duty, of other distressed persons drawn together because they

are facing the same problem, or of mixtures of such parties. The forces which accomplish the convening of the cluster can be quite variable. The signaling code which regulates and organizes the cluster apparently is one of the heritable faculties of the species.

STEP FIVE: TAKING ACTION ACCORDING TO THE SELECTED PLAN

Precept: Perseverance in a selected course of action is maintained, in the face of uncertainty over how it will "work," through use of an abiding convenant with a fixed personal decision, or as a response to a group "encouragement" instruction.

Affect-Signals: Hope, faith, resolve, "seeing it through," enduring, abiding, struggling, "hanging-in."

The central tasks of the action phase are those of doing organized work, according to a plan, often in the face of uncertainty about "how it will turn out," and in a context of unfamiliar activities and events. Up until this part of the problem-solving sequence, all has been preparatory to taking action. The steps of search, appraisal, and decision, necessary as they are, ordinarily do not yield any adaptive outcome unless there is a taking of action. The type of action undertaken, by the very nature of the presenting challenge, is often one unfamiliar to the person challenged. And its result most often cannot be securely anticipated throughout the main period of the required effort of the adaptive work. People carrying forward their plans during challenges are in the situation of Noah while he is building the ark, and while he and the ark are tumbling upon the flood waters. The appraisal of the presenting challenge has led to an action commitment which must be maintained until it is completed if it is to have any opportunity to succeed. The signaling affects marking this part of the adaptive sequence, hope, faith, and resolve, seem uniquely suited to maintaining a pattern of behavior through an interval when its effect cannot yet be known. No "outcome feedback" is possible during the very period when the new behavior is becoming organized. In this peculiar situation, resolve, faith and hope comprise a temporary variety of feedback which maintains the plan and the work of carrying it to the point where results might become visible. Although hope seems to be a fundamental requirement for carrying through prolonged adaptive efforts, its underpinnings are not yet fully described. Individuals who report losing hope also stop carrying through long or complex plans[18]. Loss of hope is one of the central features of the clinical pattern termed "depression." Depressed persons express a major abortion of their problem-solving activities, even though their faculties appear otherwise preserved, although slowed. One of the most salient features which differentiates individuals who make a successful adaptation to a massive physical injury, such as poliomyelitis, is the presence of experiences of hopefulness spaced throughout the long interval of the adaptive period[7]. One of the principle interests of the social surrounds of such persons is to elicit and react to displays of hopefulness[7]. The ability to call into mind a picture of an outcome, together with pictures of the pathway toward that outcome, seems to be intrinsic to the competent performance of long lines of purposive behavior[19]. Apparently the signaling affects of hope, faith and resolve are linked to the mechanics for maintaining such images. As affects so closely related to the effectiveness of adaptive effort, it is easy to understand why the terms for these affects are so prevalent in the folk lexicon of coping.

STEP SIX: EVALUATION OF RESULTS

Precept: Efforts to persevere continue until exhaustion or until the experience of some marker of success as moving as was the original experience of threat.

Affect-Signals: Waiting, watching, caution, testing, checking, sounding, patience.

The activities which comprise the evaluation phase have the

effect of "homing" the adaptational efforts into their objectives. There is a watchfulness for the effects of the actions undertaken and a checking of such observations against the intended outcome. Most adaptive work entails numerous modifications of approach as further information is acquired. If the action underway doesn't seem to be working, the whole problem-solving sequence automatically recycles to the beginning. Multiple runs through the search-appraisal-decision-action-evaluation sequence are much more standard than the case where the first run accomplishes a satisfactory outcome. Individuals moving through the evaluation phase characteristically are active in cross-checking their view of the results with others. "How does it look?;" "OK;" "not OK?;" and "We're not out of the woods yet, " exemplify such monitoring exchanges. Noah sent out doves on three occasions to make sure he didn't alight from the ark before he was confident his objective was reached. The efforts to start coping are so painful, and the efforts to maintain coping so arduous, that the signal to relinquish the effort must be convincing. As apparent success approaches, the decision to relax the coping effort must be faced with the same earnestness as regards possible hazards, as was the earlier decision "to face the trouble." Sometimes an individual can get distracted from noticing "how it is going" by the arduous efforts he is making; people around him may call his attention to this diversion from the task, or remind him to "Keep your eye on the ball." Other times the surrounding group will say, "Are you sure you're out of the woods?" The surround collaborates with the individual in regulating the direction, duration and precision of his efforts as the effects of his activities unfold. Cautious "watching" activity is added to the strenuous struggling efforts of the adapting person. A regulatory press on the activities of adaptation operates to maintain the effort until a satisfactory resolution unfolds, but no further.

STEP SEVEN: RETURN TO ORDINARY STATE

Precept: The costly energies and resources recruited

into the adaptational sequence must be relinquished and returned to their more usual patterns as soon as possible.

Affect-Signals: Celebration, taking pride, relaxation, taking stock.

The tasks of the closing step of the adaptational sequence center on drawing to a close a line of activity which has acquired an inherent momentum, and on quickly resuming more ordinary activities. Just as a special pattern of reckoning became established once a challenge had been detected, now the suspended but more usual pattern of reckoning will again intrude. The daily rhythms of activity resume in the context of a socially regulated transition. The individual takes pride in mastery of the challenge. The surround celebrates with him while expectantly recalling him to his standard roles. Whatever moratorium and special expectancies had been in effect are suspended as ordinary affairs resume. In the story of the ark, Noah took stock of the facts of his survival, gave thanks and planted a vineyard. The social regulation of the wind-down of the special adaptational state seems to be as automatic and intrinsic as that for its commencing. Much of the behavior and biology underlying the "switch-overs" at entry and exit of the state remain to be described. What is known suggests that the adaptational state contains substantial hazards if prolonged [20]. Bereavement can become prolonged into a state of constricted exhaustion[6]. Infants not reestablishing a renewed attachment after a critical duration of separation may permanently lose their reattachment faculty[4]. Individuals faced with repeated adaptational challenges, or challenges in tandem without an interval of repair, may acquire enduring changes of behavior and physiology which closely resemble characteristics of the adaptational state itself[21-23]. The affect of dread and the call of distress help to mobilize the behavior and cognition of the adaptive state and to recruit the social surround into its regulatory activities. Afterward, the affects of taking pride

Table 3
STEPS IN CONDUCT OF ADAPTIVE WORK

Step	Task	Activity	Affect-Signal	Activity of Surround
1. Discovery of challenge	Starting	Recruiting resources	Terror, distress call	Regulating onset
2. Recognizing problem	Surveying	Defining problem	Perplexion, anger, reminiscence, sadness	Convening, regulating, diverting
3. Constructing possibilities	Envisioning	Constructing options	Suspicion, doubt	Offering possibilities, regulating esteem and dignity
4. Selecting an action	Deciding	Comparing for value	Complaining, certitude	Pushing, testing, recollecting attachments
5. Taking action	Persevering	Working the plan	Hope, resolve	Maintaining vigil
6. Evaluating results	Testing	Detecting effect	Caution, patience	Cross-checking
7. Return to ordinary mode	Reorganizing	Establishing new patterns	Celebration, pride	Regulating relaxation

and celebrating delivery orchestrate the return to more ordinary patterns of activity.

SUMMARY

The work of meeting a challenge to an existing pattern of living follows a sequence made necessary by the logic of switching, made possible by the physiology of the crisis state, and regulated by the social surround. The activities and social domain called "helping" occur in the immediate surround of an individual passing through an adaptational episode. "Helping" is regulated by a flow of automatic signaling affects, each peculiar to a limited phase of the episode. Several dominant activities of professionals are rooted in the biologic requirement that individuals pass through adaptational episodes in a socially regulative context.

IV

SEEING IS DECIDING

The intention to help is activated by the signaling of a person in distress, and directed by observations which reveal the nature of the predicament. The full range of observations brought into play has not been systematically examined. What is known suggests that the interlockings between observing and helping can so strongly influence the situation, that they must be counted as principle governing factors.

We have earlier noted the powerful lines of behavior which flow from those who detect the fact that a person is in distress. We have considered the consequences that knowing the condition of the seven essential attachments will have on such helping behavior. These two determinations illustrate a basic class of operations—operations whose value resides in their close linkages to a strategy of helping. But the act of observing can serve many purposes besides helping, and still be set within the context of dutiful service. Let us silhouette "helpful observing" against a background of several other applications.

FIXING BY SELECTING

Observing is an activity which alters the person in distress, and the observer, in interesting ways. The observer makes decisions about whether, when and how to help on the basis of the observations he makes. The person in distress, turbulently moving across an adaptational episode without his usual psychological moorings, picks up "instructions" about who he is and what is happening from the observations passed on by those around him. All such social feedback is selective. It arises out of the act of a particular person, observing from a given vantage point, for a specific purpose. But that which the observer selects to feed back to the person, though it may be selected in the flux of a moment, can acquire a more general and more enduring life.

Consider the observations made by professional caregivers. One consequence of professional training is the acquisition of a compelling patterning to the flow of mental attention; that is, a relatively fixed set of concepts which the professional adopts, and in which he characteristically expresses confidence. Any such set of concepts, because of their influence on the flow of attention, foreshadows many later decisions and actions. Affectionate regard for tenets of theory can create an aura of significance around particular observations, and a major pressure to make decisions of enduring consequence on the most fleeting of cues. A helper can become so fixed in describing a few details that he has selected as significant on the basis of his particular theory, that he is diverted from noting other events more likely to energize his helping interest. He can get fixed on describing "what is there" without being aware that by giving "it" stable facthood he has performed an operation which greatly empowers "it." He has come upon a turbulent, flowing situation and has stabilized its social influence. Suppose he has selected that portion of a situation which fills out a picture of illness and disability. Then the social actions which follow upon observing "it" and labeling "it" have the impact of further stabilizing "it" into a drama much of whose story is fixed. The observer, whether naive or trained, cannot avoid conferring a social dynamic onto the fragments he decides to highlight and label.

Several characteristics of persons in crisis act to accentuate the impact that the perceptions of the social surround will have. Distressed persons' narrowed focus of attention can become further magnetized by whatever is impressive to their social surround. Their personal identity, diffused and lost from its moorings, is often reconstructed around the features found interesting by persons present during the heat of the challenge. What is seen is what will be made. What is noted to be developing, whether in trace or major quantities, is what will become salient. The self-identity appears not to be a fixed property of the person, but a transaction between the person and a surround. It arises from self-perceptions ane perceptions of others' perceptions. It is always partly created from expectations of the network. This intriguing set of dynamics becomes especially important during episodes of crisis, when the beliefs of care-givers sometimes comprise the dominant inputs for a future identity. The network plants what seeds may grow.

The impact of the selectivity of the observer is perhaps nowhere more heightened than in the diagnostic process. Diagnostic labels can summarize decisive facts, and are necessary for precision in the giving of help. But in the work of a portion of current mental health practitioners, labels have acquired a powerful outcome-forecasting quality, without adding much precision to the design for helping, or without being otherwise informative. The "diagnostic workup" has come to assume, in its social expression, the status of a formal forecast of outcome. The pertinent social network and the larger public regularly act as if they regard "the diagnosis" as the experts' comprehensive judgment about the events being observed. Diagnostic utterance has acquired a public dramaturgic status as a classifying label, promise and prediction, all made about a person-in-trouble.

Judge Bazelon has commented on the impact some terms used in psychiatric diagnosis have on the complex judgments that must be made in a courtroom[1]:

> In Durham v. United States, we announced a new
> test for insanity: "An accused is not criminally responsi-

ble if his unlawful act was a product of a mental disease or defect." We intended to widen the range of expert testimony in order to enable the jury "to consider information advanced by relevant scientific disciplines." This purpose was not fully achieved, largely because many people thought *Durham* was an attempt to identify a clearly defined category of persons—those classified as mentally ill by the medical profession—and excuse them from criminal responsibility . . .

The jury's wide latitude in deciding the issue of responsibility requires that judges ensure that the jury base its decision on the behavioral data which are relevant to a determination of blameworthiness . . .

We are deeply troubled by the persistent use of labels and by the paucity of meaningful information presented to the jury. Experience with the administration of the insanity defense has revealed that, despite the earnest efforts of witnesses, counsel and judges, these defects are a recurring problem . . .

The expert witnesses base their conclusions on certain studies, but they tell the jury only the conclusions without any explanation of the studies themselves, what facts the studies uncovered, and why these facts lead to the conclusions . . .

These labels and definitions are not merely uninformative. Their persistent use has served to distract the jury's attention from the few underlying facts mentioned. For example, the fact that the defendant's difficulties "in relating adequately to other people are more severe or more extreme than the average [person's]" is immersed in a dispute about whether to classify these difficulties as a "personality defect," a "personality problem," a "personality disorder," a "disease," an "illness," or simply a "type of personality."

Although this discussion of conclusory labeling is cast in the context of a courtroom inquiry, there may be parallel constrictions and diversions when these same summarizing labels intrude upon the assessment of distressed or distressing behavior in settings other than courtrooms.

Another hazard within some diagnostic systems lies in their potential for becoming unlinked from a strategy of helping, and placed into the service of "explanatory disengagement." Instead of expediting the work of deciding which kind of help would be most useful, the diagnostic labels are recruited into explaining why "nothing can be done." The most widely used medical nomenclature for classifying troubling behavior[2] is built around a list of terms that is extraordinarily powerful in predictively allocating which line of catastrophe will ensue. Most of its 44 terms are comprised of different admixtures of a set of 94 "abnormal characteristics"[3]. Because it is a logical system offering only standardized abnormal findings in differing arrangements, it can easily be used to foreshadow the type of disability state that is soon to make its presence more clearly evident. This nomenclature is a demonstrably powerful plan for simplifying data. It is quite feasible to program a computer to process the observations professionals have made regarding the 94 specified areas of observation. The machine then can arrive at diagnostic labeling which has a reliable level of agreement with the labeling applied by experienced clinicians working from the same observations[3]. A further peculiarity of this diagnostic system resides in the fact that a high percentage, perhaps half, of its "abnormal findings" are only subtly different from findings like anger, suspicion, fear and perplexity—terms which denote behavior present in all humans, especially at times of the adaptational life interval (see Chapter III). Thus we are faced with the peculiar situation that a large proportion of the professionally made observations concerning a person passing through an adaptational interval can be drawn effortlessly into the service of making predictions of his demise, or into explanations for prudent disengagement.

Because of the comforting intricacy of this system, its conclusory projections may be widely thought plausible, and the resulting inferences thought respectable. However, careful study of the application of the psychiatric diagnostic nomenclature has raised serious question as to whether it can be applied to projections of future life performance. For instance, the life status of having acquired a particular psychiatric diagnosis offers little assistance to professionals as a prediction such a person will express socially dangerous behavior[4]. And in general, later performance has no detectable relation to the attributes which qualify an individual for one or another psychiatric diagnostic term[5]. For example, investigators in military settings have repeatedly discovered that successful predictions concerning individuals who will later show poor military performance do not turn on the observations summarized in the standard psychiatric nomenclature[5]. The psychiatric nomenclature also shows a peculiar geographic variance, which may further suggest its disconnection from a strategy of helping. In day-to-day use it is applied somewhat differently by professionals trained or working in separate subcultures. For instance, in recent years, hospitalized persons who are moody and show some disorganization of thought would likely be called "schizophrenic" in New York City, but "depressed" in London[6].

But terms of classification can have dangers beyond explanatory disengagement and recruitatory prediction. They can acquire an unwarranted psychological reality. A term can become, to one who frequently employs it, the thing being treated. Whatever usefulness may derive from referring to troubled people in shorthand, as "cases" of this or "examples" of that, the practice carries risks. The shorthand term can become the object of thought and focus of decision. It can become a stylized reality, authoritatively communicated to the family and network. It can eloquently simplify the complexity in a situation but in a way so as to lose critical information. Frequent usage can lend credence to the primitive notion that the real situation is authentically described by the label. Ordinary care-giving sentiments toward the person in distress can become aborted. Sentiments shift from the person and become automatic reactions to the label. Sometimes, the network and family may come to regard the label itself as an influence in the troubled person's life—a category of influence which may be "spreading," even contagious. The label, almost automatically, can move through the serial statuses "review of key features of a person in a situation," to "shorthand description," to "the problem," to "a case of" and "you know what happens with these cases," ending with "you had better watch out for yourself near a case of." The movements from status as observation, through facthood, and on to dangerous-influence status occur partly because of the authority and expertise the professional helpers are assumed to possess. But such movement is lubricated by already powerful alienating attitudes among all the participants, both from the regular network and the temporary helper. Sometimes, in utter frustration, the participants in these tedious dramas turn to scapegoating operations of types that can be disguised from their own gaze. One handy tunnel lies within the usual patterns of labeling mental illness for quiet export to experts "for treatment." For example, "chronic" can be used as a coded label which assists the network and the helpers to collaborate in agreeing to tacitly disengage from "the problem."

Another example of unrecognized movement from observation to "fact," one even more fully unlinked from a strategy of helping, is illustrated in a study that surveyed a sample of residents of New York City in order to discover "true rates of mental illness," as distinct from treated, or serviced, illness[7]. One of the principle sources of data in this study was a series of home interviews. The interviews were conducted with 1660 adults selected because they were unknown to any psychiatric treatment facility, and were thought to comprise a cross-sectional sample of adults resident in New York. This survey by home interviews determined that only 18.5% of the sample was "well" (free of symptoms), while ratings of "marked, severe, and incapacitated" (abundant symptoms) were applied to 23.4% of the sample[7]. Persons in the home interview sample were asked whether they had experienced any of a long list of "symptoms." The experiences listed included items like "sleeplessness," "strange thoughts" and "feelings that life isn't worthwhile." The interviewed persons were also asked whether they had experienced these listed events infrequently, or frequently, in the last several months, and in the last several years. In such a procedure, the "counts of symptoms" represent a person's remembrances of experiences he regards as abnormal, with some coaching in assessing what shall be termed "abnormal." The peculiar circumstance is then operative that persons with a more efficient memory, or persons more vigorous in detecting deviations from some view of normal health, will qualify themselves for higher symptom counts. And such persons will be classified for inclusion among the "more disabled." The operation of this factor of "dutiful recall" may also help explain why the same study determined that persons of higher social status and higher education tended to have higher symptom counts[7]. Although these counts of recollections of "symptoms" were conducted to determine whether there might be a large pool of unserviced mental illness, such counts more likely demonstrate that individuals can, when asked, dutifully remember the discomforts and anguish which regularly attend ordinary episodes of adaptational work. The peculiarly high estimates of mental illness inferred from this survey also suggests the readiness in popular diagnostic practice to nimbly leap to projections of incapacity. Any scheme for gathering observations that becomes unhitched from planning how to help, can emerge, in full diagnostic regalia, as the compelling script for a long-playing tragedy.

Some of the tragic consequences that can encumber any automatic counting of supposed abnormalities are illustrated in the dreadful witchhunting episodes of the fifteenth century. During the miasma of the witchhunt, inconsequential details—such as being near a particular place or person—came to be invested with grave diagnostic significance. Experiences intrinsic to ordinary episodes of distress, like fright, could be ascribed to the influence of a witch. Passages from Kramer and Sprenger's treatise on witchcraft, *Malleus Maleficarum*, illustrate the logic of inference from trivia[8]. Because their classificatory efforts happened long ago, the absurd design and recruitatory application may be easier to appreciate. Kramer and Sprenger were asked to deal comprehensively and authoritatively with witchcraft (as reported in a Bull of Innocent VIII in 1484):

>It has lately come to our ears . . . that in some parts of the territories and dioceses . . . many persons of both sexes . . . have abandoned themselves to devils, incubi, and succubi . . . and by their incantations . . . charms, crafts . . . and horrid offenses have slain infants yet in the mother's womb, have blasted the produce of the vine . . . [and do] afflict and torment men and women with piteous pains and sore diseases . . . and hinder man from performing the sexual act . . . and are a cause of scandal and danger to very many . . . .
>
>Our dear sons Henry Kramer and James Sprenger, Professors of Theology . . . have been by letters Apostolic [made] delegates and Inquisitors of these . . . pravities . . . .
>
>Being wholly desirous of removing all hindrances . . . [to] their good work . . . we decree and enjoin that . . . the Inquisitors be empowered to proceed to the just correction, imprisonment and punishment of any persons . . . in the kind named (pp. xliij).

Following this outline of purpose, the task that emerged was to detect which persons were witches through the application of specified criteria:

>They make horses go mad under their riders . . . .
>They can affect Judges and Magistrates so they cannot hurt them . . . and bring a great trembling in the hands of those who would arrest them . . . .
>
>Doctors may perceive from the circumstances such as the complexion and the reaction of his eyes . . . that the disease does not result from a defect of the blood or the stomach or to any natural defect . . . but to an extrinsic cause . . . to witchcraft . . . .
>
>They can turn the minds of men to inordinate love or hatred.
>They can make of no effect the generative desires,

> and even the power of copulation . . . cause abortion, kill
> infants in the mother's womb . . . with a mere look . . .
> (pp. 99ff.).

The suggested classificatory system is securely comprehensive and can comfortably allocate almost any likely
observation:

> After they have confessed their crimes under torture
> they always try to hang themselves . . . (pp. 102ff.).

Because more general issues of classificatory logic were
pushed aside by urgent ideologic pressure, the experts could
apply themselves to descriptions of proper inquisitional
procedure:

> Commonest and most usual [is the situation] . . .
> when no accuser appears . . . but there is a general report
> of witchcraft in some town. . . . [So] the Judge may pro-
> cede without a general citation or admonition . . . since
> the noise of the report often first comes to his ears . . . (p.
> 207).
> If the accused says she is falsely accused it is a sign
> she is asking to defend herself . . . (p. 216).
> It is further to be noted that it is a punishable of-
> fense to publish the names of witnesses indiscretely . . .
> (p. 217).
> And while she is questioned about each several
> point, let her be often and frequently exposed to torture,
> beginning with the more gentle. But if she is not induced
> by terror to confess, the torture must be continued onto
> the second or third day . . . but not repeated [after that]
> unless there should be some fresh indication of its prob-
> able success . . . (p. 226).

Ingenious as this classificatory system may be, its pattern is
one of attaching major, conclusory importance to observations taken from the ordinary fabric of life. The frailty of its
logic is transparent to persons not burdened with the particular distractions of that age. Current diagnostic practices

are in no major way put to the same uses as were the observations which identified a witch. *But these fifteenth century
practices can alert us to the logical emptiness of any system
which can only "discover" defectiveness. Its observations,
no matter how rearranged, can only select from among a set
of catastrophes.* In addition, perhaps the situational distance
from these earlier diagnostic practices allows us to see what
their designers could not: that the observations from which
so much proceeded were trivial.

OBSERVING AND A DESIGN FOR HELP

The hazards to helping which can reside in the acts of
observing are not intrinsic. They fade to insignificance when
observation is conducted as a preparation for service activity. Observing does not lead to "fixing" the temporary
plumage of distress when the observer is working to discover the person who is struggling beneath the distress. Observing does not lead to conclusory labeling when the features
selected inform a helper which leverage points he might
employ to reestablish the conduct of the adaptational work
in process. Observation does not recruit into any sanctuarial
catastrophe when it draws its cues from a focused plan to
assist with the adaptational work at hand.

Four areas of assessment may illustrate mechanics for
linking the act of observing to the act of helping. Each of the
four kinds of information significantly alters the approach
the helpers may employ in the design of their efforts to
assist.

IS THE INDIVIDUAL EXHAUSTED? Distressed persons regularly
move into elevated levels of activity and perceptual arousal.
These high-energy states just as regularly disrupt ordinary
sleeping-waking rhythms, and lead to situations of prolonged sleeplessness and to a deep general fatigue. The resulting reductions in the effectiveness of task performance
are well-known in human experience. The physiological underpinnings of the reduced performance of the sleep-deprived

state are still being described, but enough is known to suggest the importance of relieving the condition when it becomes a factor in the conduct of adaptational work. A markedly shortened amount of sleep is an early component of several clinical problems, for instance depression and acute schizophrenia. Clinicians often note a close correlation between the normalization of sleeping patterns and an improvement in social performance among persons with schizophrenic patterns of disturbance[9]. Much significant mental reorganization of recent and past experience may, for many people, occur primarily during intervals of sleep[10]. Systematic activities designed to maintain prisoners in prolonged intervals of sleeplessness apparently are a reliable method for profoundly disorganizing their perception, cognition and performance [11/12]. Arrangements to reestablish eating, hydration and sleep are a reliable way to restore exhausted military personnel when their performance has been impaired by prolonged and sleepless exhaustion[13]. Although phenothiazine medication and transcerebral electrical stimulation are reliable methods for reinstalling normal sleeping-waking rhythms in sleepless persons[14/15], so too are exercise, warm milk, music and quiet, socially comforting situations. Thus it is important for the professional to discover whether a person active in an adaptational challenge is suffering from prolonged sleeplessness; a factor that can alter the outcome. A focused inquiry can easily detect the presence of sleeplessness. Such observation comprises a type of assessment closely linked with a strategy of enhancing adaptational work. Clinical experience suggests that sleeplessness and exhaustion frequently may be overlooked, perhaps because of the more dramatic distractions usually present during a flurry of adaptational distress.

DOES THE INDIVIDUAL CARRY THE SCHIZOPHRENIC PATTERN OF ALTERED PERFORMANCE DURING EPISODES OF DISTRESS? The life condition known as schizophrenia includes a characteristically altered pattern and duration of adaptational episodes. The resulting flow of behavior is less likely to move through the problem-solving sequence within the ordinary several-week duration of the adaptational interval. It is less likely to effectively maintain essential regulatory relationships with the social surround. A significant fraction of individuals demonstrating the schizophrenic pattern may have a genetically transmitted variety of the disorder[16-20]. Blood relatives express the disorder in a pattern suggesting an inherited difference in key biochemical systems[16-24]. The resulting pattern of inheritance is large enough to be clearly visible in analyses which move across major differences in child-rearing and life experience[17-20]. The effect may be located in systems that provide characteristic differences in the metabolic flow of materials intrinsic to the function of the synapse, e.g., neural transmitter substances such as the indolamines and catecholamines[16 21 24]. These same materials are prominently involved in the chemical events of adaptational episodes[16,21-24]. Reductions in the activity of particular enzymes, for example, dopamine-beta-hydroxylase, and elevated levels in body excretions of materials derived from the catecholamines and indolamines, such as urinary indolacetic acid and urinary vanylmandelic acid, may one day allow a convenient chemical assay for schizophrenia.

The types of observations used to detect the presence of the schizophrenic vulnerability might be biochemical assays. They might be observations of current performance, like bizarre concept formation, or hallucinations in a person who otherwise shows no loss of memory or of the ability to recognize his context in time, place and person. Or they may be historical information about prior performance in distress, or about a family pedigree revealing a characteristic distribution of the defect. The clinical importance of detecting the presence of schizophrenia lies in the fact that a greatly defective performance during adaptational episodes may be markedly improved when its biochemical underpinnings are partly controlled by phenothiazine or butyrophenone medication. A major improvement can occur in the adaptional work of schizophrenic persons when they consume the proper amounts of such materials [25].

This chemical softening of the abnormality in schizo-
phrenia can offer a noteworthy assist to the ability to con-
duct adaptational work, but such work naturally must still
be performed in the usual way. Studies of the effectiveness of
different strategies for assisting persons with the schizophrenic liability suggest that factors besides biochemical
ones can be important. For instance, a recent evolution in
clinical approach which employs institutional settings for
shorter durations has been associated with a less deteriora-
tive life course in schizophrenic persons[26]. Several social interventions, ranging from counseling to assistance in maintaining group affiliations, apparently can greatly alter the
course of the schizophrenic liability over a lifetime, and the
adaptational success during a challenge event [27-30]. A body of
experience is accruing which indicates that many categories
of assistance with the conduct of adaptational work can
have their greatest effect with simultaneous use of phenothiazine or butyrophenone medication[30]. For these several
reasons, a set of observations allowing a helper to detect the
fact that he is dealing with an individual carrying the schizophrenic liability can greatly increase the precision of his
helping efforts.

IS THE INDIVIDUAL SOCIALLY ISOLATED?   Observations which can detect the absence of individuals in the weekly flow of a person's life with whom he is regularly in contact, suggest he is
isolated. Such information is basic to arranging a useful service. A socially isolated person is missing the corporate substrate essential for particular stages in the work of adaptation (see Chapter III). An individual's friends, family, work
associates and neighbors perform activities intrinsic to managing the challenges he will face as he deals with the life
problems that brought him into service. The functions performed by a social network, one in contact and available to a
person in distress, are sufficiently vital that such a network
must be provided as an aspect of the service arrangements
when it is otherwise absent. Whether it is an individual's ordinary network, or whether a temporary one supplied in the

context of service, the network delivers a flow of regulatory actions—the effect of which is to focus the individual's special behavior and mental capacities, characteristic of the adaptational interval, onto the tasks and timing required by the current predicament. With precision and subtlety born, not so much out of affectionate regard, as of propinquity and membership in the species, the surround assists the individual to define the loss or problem, to recollect his central life concerns and to detect headway along his chosen plan of action. When the adaptational work is proceeding too slowly, the network will "push" it by trying to convert a stance of perplexity into one of decision, or a stance of complaint into one of action. If action is moving precipitously, persons in the surround will introduce more reflection. For instance, they might direct attention onto the future situations consequent to several alternate paths within the current action possibilities. Throughout the process, the surround takes other actions which maintain an individual's dignity, status and social relatedness.

A vast body of evidence has gathered to document the risks attending social isolation. Persons who are living alone, divorced, widowed, separated or migrant, are between 10 and 20 times overrepresented in psychiatric services[31-34]. Isolated persons enter all types of psychiatric services younger, stay longer and return more often than non-isolated persons[31-34]. Isolated persons also die younger from illness of many kinds, vascular, infectious and metabolic, than do persons living in a family or household unit[35]. Persons who recently have migrated, frequently leaving their social connections behind, are overrepresented in psychiatric institutions with diagnoses of many kinds, including schizophrenia, senile change, depression and alcoholism[36/37]. Spontaneous events, or administrative actions, which convene isolated persons into work groups or social groups can have profound effects in expanding their general health and social competence[38-42]. It appears that these new groups of formerly isolated persons do not have to make any special efforts to intellectually understand psychological processes in order for the performance-enhancing effects to occur[38-42]. Professionals can facilitate the formation and persistence of these new groups of formerly isolated persons in ways that do not depend upon the professional's continuing membership, presence or activity in the group[38-42].

A line of evidence concerning the clinical risks inherent in social isolation is also being gathered from the study of events at the biochemical level. Rats maintained in a state of prolonged separation from other members of the species lose a portion of their metabolic capacity to produce, use, and destroy after use key chemicals like epinephrine, norepinephrine and dopamine[21,43]. These materials are involved in responding to social stimuli, and are relevant to the conduct of adaptational work. A particular enzyme system, catechol-o-methyl-transferase, has been shown to decline, in the isolated rats, to below-normal levels of availability[21,43]. When returned to areas offering normal levels of social stimulation, such rats show a condition of disorganized hyperarousal. They also show a diminished ability to carry on the activities which regulate their position in the social hierarchy, and to organize the collaborative use of shared space[43].

Social isolation appears to constitute a catastrophic hazard, both as a continuing predicament and, especially, during episodes of adaptational work. As such, it becomes a basic clinical fact that must be discovered when present. Observations which review a person's remembrances of social contacts over a recent day or week can ascertain the existence of a network of persons. Some people's signaling may be impaired. Some networks are preoccupied. The available network may for some reason not become drawn into the current adaptational work. The signaling and responding must be assessed. Is the network aware of the individual's signals of distress? Is the network responding to such signals with movement toward, or away, from the individual? If members of the network are asked to assemble to conduct some aspect of activities to help the individual, do they convene or do they distance themselves? The reactivity and convenability of an individual's network constitute basic information for developing responsive services. The observations which yield such information are ordinarily easily available, especially when the observer makes provision to concentrate his attention on gathering them.

IS THE INDIVIDUAL A HEAVY OR REPEATING USER OF SERVICES? One of the most stable observations about users of psychiatric service is that individuals with a history of prolonged or repeating use of service will tend to make heavier current and future use of services. For example, of all persons admitted to residential inpatient psychiatric hospital service, approximately two-thirds (and largely single-episode users) are discharged within one year from admission. But among those who stay more than one year, many are heavy users of services, and the overall likelihood of discharge in the next year is under 20 percent. For those who stay longer than five years, the likelihood of discharge within the next year is under five percent[33,44-47]. In addition, persons presenting in other psychiatric services show a heavy concentration of previous users. Although less than 10 percent of the residents of a particular settlement will use psychiatric services even once in a lifetime, more than 20 percent of those who appear at a reception service on an average day are previous users[31-34]. More than 30 percent of those entering outpatient care are previous users[31-34]. Of those entering inpatient care, over 40 percent are previous users[31-34]. Of those who stay more than a year, more than 60 percent are previous users[31-34]. Some of this tendency for known psychiatric service users to "collect" in the system likely represents a picture of several episodic uses of service within the context of a life-long, or continuing, condition (or one which carries a risk of multiple episodes of disablement). But a number of observers suspect that other factors also make a contribution[26-29,47/48]. For instance, although a major fraction of those who collect in the care system represent the heritable, life-long biochemical abnormality which underlies clinical schizophrenia, the rate and magnitude of "schizophrenic deterioration," over a lifetime, have been observed to have markedly lessened in recent decades[26,28,48]. Since the biochemical predisposition likely remains unaffected, such reductions in rates of deterioration probably reflect some result of these changed patterns of service. Schizophrenics who are also migrants are markedly overrepresented among heavy users[36,37]. Among schizophrenics, as well as among many other groups, there is an excess of new entrants, and re-entrants, into psychiatric service during times when the general level of communal unemployment increases[56]. Schizophrenics, along with others who live in those settlements which offer more abundant outpatient services, make fewer and shorter usage of inpatient service[49-51,53]. Schizophrenics, as well as others, who live in those settlements where an individual is likely to enter the system through a reception service, one equipped to offer prompt assistance in current adaptational work, are likely to make distinctly less use of both outpatient and inpatient service[54,55]. Perhaps these observations can be summarized as a decreasing tendency for professionals to offer asylum to heavy users. They are more likely to organize themselves to offer precise assistance to persons passing through challenging adaptational episodes. Perhaps, since these episodes of service are shorter, and conducted within ordinary life settings, there may be less likelihood that a person so serviced will enlarge any existing identity or role as a patient. A focus on the adaptational work at hand may soften the lurking recruitatory effects at each episode of service.

The making of observations which can detect a known or likely user has become central in clinical practice. The utility of this pivotal assessment arises out of the magnitude of the differences in approach between serving single-episode users and serving multiple-episode users. Among the heavy users are many schizophrenics who may benefit from continued or episodic use of phenothiazine medication, but who have not been taught how to use such medication precisely. Since no continuing arrangements for use have been established, they periodically present themselves, with uncontrolled adaptational episodes, for control by hospitalization. Migrant and socially isolated persons can reduce their need for prolonged sanctuary by the use of services which help them develop newly active social affiliations[38-42]. Heavy users can benefit from services which help them put aside their recent offensive reputations and constrictive personal views of themselves[47,57/58]. They can conduct ordinary problem-solving activity[27,30], and make consequent reductions in their use of continuous clinical care[27,28,30,47,48,55]. But, although the heavy user of service can be converted to an episodic user, with major intervals during which he is away from service contact, he remains more likely to re-enter service than is average for his age and community[31-33]. Clinical arrangements for expeditious and precise re-entry may assist in minimizing the disruption to ordinary life[52], and prevent acquisition of disastrous social reputations. The clinical usefulness of detecting the heavy user lies in the consequent ability to increase the pace and precision of the current episode of service. The fleeting few weeks of the current adaptational interval need not be consumed in rediscovering a recurring pattern. The focus of service can move right to the heart of a strategy designed to assist in the conduct of the adaptational work at hand.

SUMMARY

Helping proceeds from signals which, in the main, are sent automatically and decoded by faculties which give almost no glimpse into their codes or operations. Helping activities possess a degree of biologic necessity so vital as to preclude their ordinarily being dependent upon, or regulated by, such mental states as might be acquired through any cultural learning.

But helping activities can be deflected from their usual purposes by several categories of notions which transform distress-signaling into hazard-signaling. The person-in-distress can so be converted into a "hazardous object" by subtle losses of signalings, such as those that are seen in courtroom proceedings or diagnostic rituals. Technical experts can lose the message of distress within an analysis of trivial detail. But there is no intrinsic reason why technical assessments of the predicament of a troubled person need obscure the primary and vital activities of signaling.

The assessment patterns most likely to interfere with the adaptational signaling in process are those organized around "explanatory disengagement," or patterns comprised only of rearrangements among narrow sets of "hazardous findings." But, more generally, any scheme for gathering observations which becomes unhitched from planning how to help, can emerge, in full diagnostic regalia, as the compelling script for a longplaying tragedy.

Observations flowing from some picture of the mechanics of adaptation may offer more likelihood of adding to the precision of helpers. *When there is exhaustion,* rest can change the picture. *When there is schizophrenia (restricted catecholamine kinetics),* phenothiazines can lay the base for conducting ordinary adaptational work. *When there is social isolation,* new affiliations and an interim social context breathe desire and pattern into efforts at coping. *When there has been previous heavy service,* a fast drive to the heart of the problem can reduce the risks of recruitment into patienthood roles, and into the convoluted social networks of treatment.

V

RECEPTION SERVICE

BEGINNING AT THE BEGINNING

As the mechanics of adaptational work become better understood, helping services are able to shed some less productive practices. Recent advances in the appreciation of the regulatory interplay between a struggling person and the helping activities of those around portend the emergence of a strikingly more precise concept of "service." The process of entry into professional service has been revealed to embody a complex social domain, one governed by factors seldom discussed even a decade ago. Most particularly, recent service designs show a distinctive focus on the events of the first several hours of service. These practices often go by the term "reception services," because the activities attendant upon the process of reception appear to possess a general and previously unsuspected potential for restarting an individual's adaptational work when it has become aborted or has lost stride.

It has not always been so. The earlier term, "intake service," referred to a set of activities considered to ensue before the "real service" began. The main purpose behind such intake proceedings was to sift and sort out those individuals who were thought to qualify for the services offered by a particular set of practitioners. The intake personnel would ask questions such as these: What type of distress or symptoms does the individual express (alcoholism, school phobia, delusions)? What demographic characteristics does he represent (age, sex, marital status, financial resources, religious affiliation, locale of residence)? What issues of jurisprudence effect his status (proceedings for commitment to hospitalization, divorce proceedings, court-ordered assessments of behavior, truancy charges)? What interest does the individual express in receiving the services in question, as he may understand them ("motivation," "readiness," "workability," "likely to do well")? These early observations would be summarized at a staff conference centered on the task of deciding whether to admit to service. The qualifying procedure regularly consumed several staff days of "pre-service" activity. This "pre-service" concept was also expressed in the fact that a decision in the affirmative, "an intake," routinely led, not to a starting of service, but to placement on a waiting list, sometimes for weeks or months, while awaiting "a treatment hour opening." Individuals found "not suitable" for services of the agency might be referred to "a more appropriate agency." At this next stop, the individual might undergo a duplicative "intake study." Afterwards, he might again be placed onto a waiting list or again designated for further referral.

This style of reception activities is rapidly fading from American practice. It would not warrant current discussion except for some incidental discoveries of continuing importance. Out of such beginnings emerged the fact that many agencies were organized to provide a narrow, "sectoral," range of services, but were faced with service users seeming to call for a "package" of several services.[1,8] Such practices also made visible the frequent occurrence during service of some intriguing changes in the basic social affiliations of patients. All too often, and especially in major grades of distress, the individual permanently shifted his affiliations from ordinary social networks, composed of family, friends and associates, to another social system, mainly composed of treatment figures. This shift of affiliations was discovered to occasionally occur with alarming speed. What emerged was a systematic pattern of reaffiliation—to new persons (healers, doctors), new roles (patienthood), new reputations (stigma), new locations (hospitals, clinics), new codes of behavior ("understanding," "psychopathology") and a new explanatory rhetoric ("chronicity," "schizophrenogenic mother").[2-6]

This originally perplexing entry-to-service behavior has more recently been recognized as comprising an orderly social domain, one having the effect of regulating the contact between two usually separated, often quite different, social systems. The effect of such regulation is to maintain an individual's membership in his ordinary and persisting network, thus to limit his recruitment into the accessory network of the helpers. At the zone of contact between the two systems occur varying amounts of merger by temporary cooperation, mingling by the interplay of roles, and exchange by signals and information. Most individuals report the crossing of this zone, the entrance experience, as a turbulent one. "Entry into service," or commencement of more-than-momentary contact with professional helpers, is a category of personal problem which few individuals seem able to manage smoothly. The entering person negotiates his entry into an unfamiliar terrain at the very time that he is especially preoccupied with anguish, and likely to be performing below his more usual levels. The resulting turbulence affects more people than the main figures alone. The events at the zone of contact flow chaotically across the lives of several people in both systems. The ability of the individual to maintain the ordinary lines of behavior which attach him to a family and community fades during the very interval when entry into service usually occurs (see Chapter I). The friendly guidance which an individual might find useful while reconnoitering an unfamiliar domain typically falters as a sideplay in the spread of adaptational disturbance.

Consequent to this beginning understanding of some regularities in the turbulence at reception, some surprises have emerged. Generally unsuspected was the fact that the events at reception were occupying a heavy proportion of the labor of professional helpers. This activity, formerly thought incidental and "before" service proper, in fact consumed one-third to one-half of the contact time of the helpers. This major volume of activity took place almost casually, in settings designed for something quite different. Turbulently textured group business struggled along in rooms equipped for private conversation between two thoughtful persons at an appointed hour. The decisions which defined an entire episode of service were squeezed between appointments, in the hallway, and conducted without the presence of the principal parties.

However, experience has now shown that the hours of service immediately following contact are invested with an altogether unexpected clinical importance. It has repeatedly, and unavoidably, been observed that some of the most persisting clinical changes often occur "before the service begins." Individuals presenting with the full plumage of crisis not uncommonly start their adaptational work at once—during the presumably "preliminary" inquiry to determine whether an intake should be made. The family sentiments and roles change to a greater extent during the initial hours of contact, than later when the treatment strategy proper has been decided. On the other hand, some persons who entered the intake proceedings ready for problem-solving, actively perplexed about what to do about their difficulties, quickly relieved themselves of such quandary as they discovered that the therapists "would be directing the treatment." The intake proceeding seemed to carry with it an unexplained ability to turn the adaptational process on and off, and do it quickly—while being conducted as if it were merely incidental to the real services. In recent years, the outlines of the brief few weeks of the adaptational state everywhere presented these mysteries.[7-9] The behavior and physiology of the adaptational state appear more and more to account for the surprises and mysteries attending the early phases of service. And the interval of the intake process, because it was that portion of professional contact so timed as to be likely to occur during the evanescent adaptational state, moved from "before service" to "the beginning of service."

PROFESSIONAL TASKS AT RECEPTION

ARRANGING FOR A SOCIAL CONTEXT: THE CORE OF THE PROCESS OF RECEPTION   The term "social regulation," as applied to the adaptational work of individuals presenting for service during a challenge, refers to the effects persons surrounding the challenged individual have on such work. The axioms in Chapters I and III summarize several of these consequences. For instance, the adaptational work of individuals who are isolated from a social surround tends to become prolonged or diffused. It may not get started in the first place. Because of the essential nature of the activities of the social surround, professional practices which provide one when it is absent, or convene one when it is fragmented, dominate the work of reception. Professional effort centers on insuring a range of social contacts which will affect the adaptational work in process through semi-automatic pacing and focusing responses.

Of similar importance are efforts directed to protecting the nervous system, the basic machinery of adaptation, from known hazards. For example, modern reception practices avoid the use of particular medications which relieve distress, but which also soften or modify the emotional states characteristic of adaptational activity. Such emotions comprise a signalling system through which an individual coordinates the pace of his efforts with activities arising in the social surround (see Chapter III).

Modern reception practices similarly avoid providing, even foreshadowing, the removal of an individual to a separated, sheltered space as a pathway toward relief. The earlier practices which offered sanctuary were successful in reducing a flurry of distress, but all too often aborted the adaptational work in process. Sanctuarial beckoning can consume the fleeting moments of the adaptational interval, and may teach a pattern which can lay the groundwork for future activities in pursuit of asylum.

The activities at reception which arrange the social substrate for adaptational work form a growth-edge in recent service designs. For the most part, such activities enlarge the sending or receiving of signals, or advance the general interplay between the individual and a surrounding group during an adaptational sequence. Examples of such activities would include the following:

Activating the "scanning" property of attention: diverting persons from a topic-of-choice or behavior-of-choice; diverting attention toward "problem" identification, survey of facts, discovery of more interesting lines of inquiry;

Convening fragmenting networks: families, friends, work associates, *ad hoc* groupings which can provide immediate social attachments and establish a regulative context for pending adaptational work;

Providing task definitions: timing, setting, sequencing, markers of headway, to individuals experiencing the "whir and blur" of panic, anguish and disorganization;

Assisting socially isolated persons to form new social affiliations with speed and reliability; suggesting a helping, problem-solving orientation to such task-groups;

Forming a particular category of social relationship which is focused on detecting personality, capacity for performance and aspirations (through the noise and static of symptoms and distress behavior);

Facilitating decision and action by the use of a category of counseling which works to identify disrupted attachments, assemble reminiscences of self into a clear notion, compare decision options against a description of the self and the comprehensive system of meaning, and to test the decision by taking action;

Converting several kinds of aborted decision activity into forms useful in problem-solving work: converting laundry lists of complaints into specifications of excellence; converting elusive and multivalent appraisals of situations into the best, current decision; converting general objectives into a series of detectable, testable steps; converting anger, perplexity and anguish into decisions to acquire new skills or behaviors;

Converting requests for shelter and presentations of signals of distress into plans with specific objectives and expected transit-times in service;

Derecruiting from the sick role individuals who have adopted it for imprecise objectives or extended intervals of time.

Note particularly that these activities center on facilitating the ordinary activities comprising any adaptational episode. Modern concepts of reception anticipate that the human adaptational system has powerful biologic roots, is by no means fragile, and will proceed if a few mechanics are insured. Modern reception practices also strive to insure that no line of activity will displace the prompt commencement of adaptational work, and that no professional presence will eclipse that of persisting members of an individual's social network.

The process of movement into mental health services typically occurs at a time when there is strain on an altered set of relationships within an individual's usual social network. Entry into the temporary social network of treatment also happens at a time when, characteristic of persons crossing the crisis interval, affiliative activity is exquisitely heightened. Because reception service is placed at the interface between the persisting personal network and the temporary treatment network, it acquires a gating function. It regulates recruitment into the latter by enhancing the activity of the former. Actions which draw people together into task-groups comprise a principal form of such interface gating. Such practices are prominent in many cultures. One of the most distinctive regularities of cross-cultural comparisons is the linkage between crisis-management, and activities directed toward the convening of networks [10-14] , e.g., at wakes or around the sickbed. In many cultures, the family of the person-in-distress is assembled at the time of an illness to participate in the assessment of the situation. Family members are provided opportunities to carry on tasks deemed intrinsic to the recovery of the afflicted. In this way, a renewal of attachments is fostered at a time when such attachments otherwise might falter. The cultural universality of practices which draw social networks together in situations such as illness and death suggests that network connectedness is of major importance in effecting the survival of the human species. The basic contribution to survival of such social connectedness is expressed not only in the biologic patterns for procreation, nurturance and recreation, but also in social customs which provide for convenings at crises. At its base, the importance of convening, whether by custom or professional action, resides in the utility of assuring the availability of a regulative context for individual adaptational work. Regarding their effectiveness in regulating adaptational work, we really don't know whether "organic" groups, i.e., groups arranged by kin, clan or custom, have advantages over "artificial" ones, i.e., groups convened by professionals. What we do know is that the adaptational work done without either type of social context is greatly inferior.

It is therefore understandable why convening activities are prominent in professional reception. Some of these efforts aim to draw people together into temporary task-groups. Others are directed toward re-attaching an individual to a loosening network. Although generally the signaling during an adaptational interval results in a convening and embrace, sometimes it does not. The characteristic random or unpredictable behavior of an individual-in-crisis sometimes leads to vigorous attempts to extrude him from his context. The resulting personal experience of alienation can raise already powerful attempts to attach to additional strength. Also, persons at crisis can profoundly lose contact with a sense of identity, or with any experience of meaning. In consequence, they can acquire an exquisite sensitivity to the surrounding field of signals and its messages concerning who they are and what are their life directions. Persons at crisis sometimes experience such a distressing loss of their moorings to identity and role, that they readily accept the identity of casualty and the role of mental patient. Although mental patienthood does not entail a high status, it does convey a measure of social definition and offer the dignity of a status "above zero." For all these reasons, efforts which draw together a previously dispersed network can provide an immediate basis for repairing long-time attachments, and a resulting reduction in affiliational activity toward the temporary figures of treatment.

There are problems to be faced in developing reliable convening practices. The unmanaged distress of any individual generates distress in other members of his family unit, often resulting in psychosomatic symptoms or in deteriorated role performance in many members of the unit.[15-17] Consequently, the family members may be adaptationally overextended. Such a fact has often led professionals to separate a distressing member from the rest of his family. Nevertheless, the major strategy emphasizes convening rather than separating. This is necessarily so because separating may reduce distress but if it yields an isolated person, it yields an adaptationally incompetent person. Beyond this, a convened network has greater capacity to undergo coordinate changes in its members. The members can perceive new issues more easily when assembled, than can the same group when in a dispersed condition. Professionals, even only briefly present, often put forth quite different patterns of curiosity and focus. The novelty and utility of these views often yields a shift in the perceptual categories within which current experience is registered[18]. Also, the challenged individual frequently offers new behavior within the context of a newly reassembled network. In a convened status, the network can experiment with new attitudes about the person-in-distress, and can experience a renewed engagement with the satisfactions of corporate adaptational work.

The more volatile or offensive the individual's recent

behavior has been, the more turbulent will be the network during attempts to convene it. The wish to exclude, which may recently have been focused on the troubled person, often shifts toward the individual trying to convene that network. Any person who tries to hold such an assembly in contact may experience strident signaling to desist. If the convener tries to do battle with this extrusive sentiment, it often increases. But if the convener moves gracefully through the "negative feelings" that have been redirected toward him, keeping his attention focused on efforts to specify the persisting problems for which responses are not yet developed, the energy of the network may begin to move toward the problem-solving sequences which always are lying in wait. It is a curious fact that many people have been institutionalized because the professional trouble-managers did not have any method available for dealing with alienating attitudes that had been redirected from the person-in-trouble toward them. The alienating sentiment that arose in the network then elicited in the professional a tendency either to withdraw from the situation, or to remove the troubling person from that network.

An effective convening format includes the person-in-trouble, plus three or four key figures. Those persons who are regularly part of the network, but are reluctant to be convened, are particularly important. Reluctant network figures often have informative experience with the offensive behavior of the troubled person. When included, they may report potential circumstances which, should they occur, might soften the extrusive sentiments. Conversely, the network has reduced capacity for coordinate change if pertinent but reluctant members are not convened.

A style of conducting business which draws attention toward figuring paths to useful action seems to raise more inventive capacity than does a focus on causes. Sometimes it is useful to label the troubled person's crisis behavior a "marker" that "important matters are not being satisfactorily handled." Questions that focus on "when and how" the troubled person can return to ordinary life sometimes elicit the curiosity and ingenuity of the group. Expectations for a return to function can be activated, even if they have been absent for a long time. The members' simultaneous experience of a shared signaling field, especially in the context of the crisis interval, carries a powerful dynamic for initiating even long-suspended adaptational activity.

Convened groupings approach problem-solving much the way as does an individual. The sequence starts with a search for figure and ground, problem and options. Soon the group attempts to distinguish the best action path. The troubled individual and the social surround partake of an exchange within a semi-automatic momentum. Seldom do the participants act as if they are aware of the process or sequence. Often they appear to become engaged in the process much more deeply than might have been predicted from their early reluctance. When they reach what they recognize as a proper product, they will disengage or pace themselves into next-step movements.

Successful professional conduct of convening seems to call for basic attitudes that confidently appreciate a degree of capacity that the participants have often not yet expressed. Successful convening cannot be accomplished, for instance, if the family members are regarded as "bad" or as "the cause of the trouble," or if home is seen as "the place where he got this way." The family picks up such attitudes from institutional operations as they move through its spaces. The family reacts to such signaling. Notions about "the bad mother," "the bad family," and "the place where he got this way" sometimes are prominent in professional helpers' thoughts, often expressed with major degrees of conviction and certitude. Little of such thinking can survive examination against the conventions of science. But such notions do greatly color relations between some types of temporary treatment networks and their surrounding, more ordinary, networks. It is difficult for some professional helpers to imagine that the ordinary network can act in anything other than destructive ways, let alone in ways that are essential to a constructive result. Professionals who assume a lack of constructive capacity in the ordinary network exert a power-ful constraint on adaptive change. This constraint arises because signals of futility or ineptitude get in the way of the convening and task-focusing that are preconditions to the regulatory actions of the network. Professional helpers can, on the other hand, express by manner and action their ex-pectation that the social network is quite able to proceed with its ordinary helping functions. However, the notions which some professionals offer, concerning special, toxic re-lationships in certain families, have sometimes operated to promote further separation. Separation and enclosure then yield their own consequences, which in outward appearance confirm the earlier assessments. It seems likely that terms like "bad mother" and "bad family" flow from poorly tested notions which express the extrusive sentiments of an ob-server, who, though a professional, is far from immune to the effects of urgent signaling by members of his species. Ex-trusive sentiments originate as a response to distress signal-ing of a single person but, if prolonged beyond several weeks, spread through many members of a family or other social unit. Often by the time professionals are called in, the distress signaling involves the whole unit with great in-tensity and has the consequence of stimulating professionals to experience considerable personal discomfort. Occasional-ly, the professional responds to this discomfort by with-drawing, by moving to separate the primary, distressing sig-naler from the "bad family," or to separate several members, for instance, "the bad mother." In many situations, the short-run effects of such separations are quite gratifying to all concerned.

When a professional helper confirms by his actions the extrusive sentiments that are already present in the net-work, people in the surround may voice an "Isn't it too bad," but do not seem surprised. They appear relieved and express gratitude. But the longer-run hazards of having promoted the social isolation of a person in distress have not become evi-dent to the participants. The professional who looks ahead to this second level of risk is more reluctant to collaborate in the making of expensive, short-run gains. He is more interested in keeping the short-range situation moving toward a resolution that does not expose new risks.

Pursuing a balance of long- and short-run objectives, he may convey attitudes of amazement, doubt, or perplexity in the context of requests to separate one of the members. Such attitudes keep the situations open for adaptive change in the whole unit rather than in just a part of the unit. The professional may decide to apply his signaling faculties quite directively, so as to improve the possibilities for growth. He may come upon a situation in which the social network has already begun to organize around an individual, using attitudes conventional to the sick role. The professional may direct his actions toward loosening the beginning attachments to this role, because of its longer-term risks.

Such directive action results from an awareness that inherent in the sick role are both assets and risks. The sick role carries a temporary moratorium from usual responsibilities, and offers compelling advantages in the case of acute physical illness, such as a broken limb or infection. From the tissue standpoint, for instance, the reduced activity levels within such a moratorium allow metabolic reserves to be focused on energy-consuming, healing processes. From the social point of view, the moratorium allows a person to receive help from those around him without losing dignity or interfering with self-esteem. The sick role carries a socially recognized status, as long as it is brief and associated with an expectation of early return to conventional duties. But grave risks are encountered when essential components of the individual's central adaptational ability are labeled as "sick." When the label on a disability process is not applied to a limited process, such as an infection or broken limb, but to a more general disturbance, such as problem-solving, it has the effect of tampering with the social dynamics of dignity and identity. In such a circumstance, the labeler is regarded as having defined an aspect of identity, and of having made a prediction concerning future performance. Even in the situation of a long physical illness, as for example, with chronic heart disease, the individual maintains an identity separate from that of casualty only if he maintains most or essential parts of his ordinary roles. The general moratorium, if prolonged beyond "a brief episode," always acquires a social momentum toward a redefined personal identity.

The professional can loosen extruding attitudes by suggesting that several outcomes, including resolutions unrelated to the sick role, are possible. He can raise doubt that the individual will nessarily remain in his current condition. He may suggest that persons facing challenges sometimes move to new levels of growth and skill.[9] Even signaling one's doubt about the certainty of a particular outcome can create constructive "loosening" within a network which had previously become stabilized. The very fact that the professional's predictions do not accord with the predictions of the rest of the network, appears to set up a lubricative tension which can open closed questions. The professional can mention possible circumstances which, should they occur, would promote a good outcome. The interesting set of affairs is then established that the action of the care-giver, in focusing attention on the several possible outcomes, actually operates to alter the likelihoods of these various outcomes. Such activities can put the helper in the position of eliciting from the network actions which can enhance the better resolution he traditionally strives to accomplish.[9]

Equally as productive as the convening of family networks is the convening of agency networks. Activities which bring together several types of service staff at reception appear to generously repay their costs. Heavy users of service ordinarily use clusters of several types of service. For example, they may need job training together with counseling. Additionally, they may need butyrophenone or phenothiazine medication for the biochemical component of schizophrenia. The parts of such a package of services can be assembled with somewhat more ease at reception than later. In another type of situation, several members of the family may be entering at the same time. Convening the family together with the several engaged agencies makes possible a precision and speed otherwise missing, as was discussed earlier. The several services, whether simultaneous or sequential, often reach their best levels of effectiveness when conducted in a coordinate manner, and set in phase with the pattern-erasing physiology of the adaptational interval.

MANAGING A TURBULENT OR VIOLENT RECEPTION PERIOD   Behavior characteristic of the adaptational state includes major flurries of such unlearned, automatic patterns as fighting, fleeing, attaching and hiding. The social reactions to intense distress-signaling and deterioration of role performance add to the turbulence of the situation. When the recent behavior of the distressed person has included distinct attacks against his own body, or against those of other persons, the activities at reception acquire an accelerated, even resuscitational pace —and this is not at all uncommon. Because the recent behavior of the distressed person has not infrequently included illegal conduct, local reception work routinely meshes with activity of the police and courts. These fairly common occurrences at the time of reception require responses with a range and speed that are otherwise seldom called for in mental health services.

The situation is further burdened by the severity of the consequences of several kinds of error. Life may be at risk as a consequence of a suicide attempt—for instance, by wound or poisoning. Reputation may be at risk from recent role performance, or from offensive public conduct. Job or domestic affiliations may be at risk from some behavioral consequences of untreated schizophrenia. The future integrity of the personal identity or of problem-solving skills may be at risk because of the distracting or recruitatory nature of the current behavior. Finally, adaptational competence may be at risk because the reception service where an individual happens to land is equipped to handle resuscitation but not social isolation, or to handle violence but not withdrawal from an abused chemical.

The twin requirements to act swiftly enough to preserve

life, and precisely enough to maintain the flow of adaptational work, combine to create in reception service a technically
challenging situation. The aspects of the work which call for
swift action revolve around stopping bleeding, countering
chemicals and poisons, repairing the effects of bodily violence and applying medical service to dramatic alterations in
physiologic health. These emergency reception activities situate themselves most comfortably in a hospital setting. They
take added vitality from tight linkages with ambulance and
resuscitational services, as well as with police and radio
communications. The vast bulk of this urgently-paced service is completed within several hours of the first contact.
This fact nicely provides for the feasibility of an almost immediate shift into services that are somewhat more slowly
paced, and that are designed to enhance the performance of
pending adaptational work. Services such as convening family networks, providing groups for isolated persons, regulating the onset, pace and focus of problem-solving, and insti-
tuting phenothiazine therapy for schizophrenic persons, are
of a type which can ordinarily begin in the hours immediately following such resuscitative action.

Such a prompt-onset approach to adaptational services,
beginning while still in the context of an emergency, is one of
the stronger trends in recent designs for service. A high percentage of persons thus serviced make a rapid start on problem-solving work, and tend to make major improvements in
their effectiveness and comfort.[19] For many individuals who
make such adaptive headway, the emergency context offers a
major "unfreezing" potential not seen in the older forms of
"scheduled" service.[20] In fact the "descheduled" and "walk-
in" features of such service appear to enhance the productivity of human services to a surprising extent.[21/22] Much of the
earlier professional reluctance to arrange for walk-in and 24-
hour service fades when effective linkages with local resuscitational services fall into place. Further interest in professional service that can go into operation quite early in the
turbulent phase is blossoming, as local experience with such
practices accumulates. For example, although each case of

such service is unscheduled, the daily, or annual, volume and composition of such events prove to be reasonably regular. Also, most turbulence that is severe enough to reach combative or assaultive levels is quite brief, and almost never results in injury to service staff.[21/22] Much of it results from panic, toxic, seizure and injury conditions that are soon managed.[21] About one-tenth of the persons presenting in unscheduled circumstances turn out later to be schizophrenic, and perhaps one-third of these have not been treated previously.[22]

Linkage with a "holding area," i.e., an area for observation of a situation over several hours without admitting the person into a particular, continuing type of service, usually an area immediately adjacent to the reception space, adds significantly to the service resources which can be harnessed. The availability of an area equipped for such brief holding markedly reduces the later use of inpatient service.[23] A holding area allows a more prolonged reception interval within which to accomplish, for instance, especially perplexing problems in observing or convening, or in withdrawing an individual from a chemical. A holding area is particularly helpful in dealing with children who present under turbulent circumstances.[24]

An additional measure of ability to convert turbulent episodes to successful adaptational work appears when the mental health service staff can go to the place where an emergency is occurring. Such service activity at the site of turbulent events, offered in close relation with other ambulance staff, is regular practice, for instance, in parts of the Netherlands[25] and the Soviet Union.[26] Mobility can add significantly to the precision of reception activities. If reception staff can go to the jail, hospital receiving room, nursing home, or to an individual's place of residence, many more relevant persons are available to be convened, and many more relevant facts are available for assessment. The more an individual is known to be a heavy user of services, the more it may be useful to assess him in a setting other than a hospital or clinic. The behavior such an individual offers at reception service conducted in a hospital or clinic may represent an unusually disorganized or atypical view. Several centers have found that when reception is conducted through a home visit, opportunities to attempt home care or to use non-institutional settings seem more obvious. Reception and assessment practices tightly restricted to hospital settings appear to narrow the range of settings selected for the subsequent services. Any individual-in-distress, if in enough distress, will present whatever behavior he discovers will generate access to service. Troubled persons are exquisitely sensitive to cues which suggest "the signals for entrance." They engage in signaling of whatever nature will gain the helpful services of these nice people in this place. Mobile reception and home-visiting practices can set aside the need for much of this signaling, because the "reaching out" message has already been established.

The greater the extent to which reception procedures signal they are no longer considering whether the individual qualifies for service, the more information can be developed about what kind of service would be most helpful. The earlier type of "intake service," discussed above, emphasized the question, "Is this person going to enter service here?" The most competent answer of a deeply distressed person, and the one most often offered, was a response that displayed an adaptational plumage that would elicit the answer, "Yes, an intake will occur here." To the degree that reception practices unambiguously shift the focus to the question of, "what is our best beginning?", the more the individual will be free to relinquish a display of "intake plumage."

A NOTE ON SPACE AND HELPING STRATEGY

Reception activities present space requirements that are somewhat different from the activities for which many service spaces were originally conceived. A brief look at some of these problems can suggest the nature of the remedies that are now widely in use. Reception work entails a reliable ca-

pacity to convene assemblies of people for time-limited
tasks. Activities directed toward bringing together 10-to-15
people is a category of business distinctly assisted by space
that can accommodate an assembly of such size. Because service space was typically designed around a two-person format of business, this has sometimes greatly hampered local
efforts at reception work. Some reception spaces have been
squeezed into ill-fitting quarters like hallways and waiting
rooms. A physical space organized to receive a whole family
in a dignified manner, and draw them into task-work around
a table, can enhance the success of convening. The ability to
hold a directive discussion in a room, with privacy and order, is intrinsic to the task.

A set of comfortable conventions is similarly useful for
the focused conduct of reception work. That is, the professional helper is often most helpful if he has worked out a
stable format of approach that can offer a task-centering
structure to the turbulence inherent in any emergency. Professionals who work in reception settings appear better able
to detect the real identity and personality of the person passing through the episode of distress, if there is a problem-
framing regularity to their inquiry. A step-by-step pattern to
the conduct of the assessment also adds a surprising surge of
task-directedness to the efforts of those in distress. An individual, entering in turbulence, anguished and suspicious,
regularly undergoes a constructive attitudinal change as he
moves into a space and discovers he is in the presence of
several people who seem to know what they're doing. They
meet him with informative instructions. "Glad you're here."
"Let us get started by selecting a schedule for our tasks."
"Who is with you?" "Let us move into the Planning Room and
see if we can figure a line of action which offers promise as a
way for you to handle this situation." When the process of
receiving persons-in-distress is conducted with orderly, attractive conventions, the onset and pace of adaptive work
become accelerated. The scale of these increments is sufficient to warrant professional interest in the use of regulariz-
ing formats as a basic tool.

A format of reception practices which can quickly signal a set of outcome possibilities, can further accelerate the rate of adaptational work. For instance, the individual may be a multiple-user, and may have acquired a set of habits as to how one acts in a mental health service. His ideas of "what it's like to be a patient" may encourage him to desist from his efforts to cope. They may instruct him to "try to discover what is wrong with himself." His expectations may foreshadow retreat to a cloistered environment.[27/28] These sentiments are residues of an earlier, sanctuarial style of helping (see Chapter VI), and may interfere with the conduct of the current work of adaptation.[29-31]

A general posture that endorses efficient and decisive action on pending problems can be signalled by means of the style of the procedures of reception. For example, it is useful to set "target dates" for the accomplishment of tasks. "This is what you are likely to have completed within three weeks." The description of a series of steps, with a schedule for the pace, is most regulative when offered without diffidence. There is usually more than enough uncertainty in the situation. And a schedule acts to start the work and the flow of consequences which will later resolve many of the unknowns. During the events of reception, the family is asking strategic questions, often silently. "Are we bringing George here for 15 minutes or 15 years?" During the turbulence of reception the situation is still uncertain as to whether the family will disengage, or will stay and work. The person-in-distress is still flexible as to whether he will seek sanctuary, and wait for 25 milligrams, or direct himself to the rediscovery of his life objectives. In this period of incertitude, consider the impact it will have on the person and his family to hear the people at reception say, "We're glad to have you here (because very likely some good things are going to happen)." "This is our job (and we like it and do it pretty well)." "This is the schedule (for the satisfying work you will accomplish with our help)." "In seven days we will all get together (and take satisfaction in our efforts)." A style of reception which directs itself toward specific purposes, with a specific schedule and pace, regularly has the effect of elevating the expectations of all participants. It engages the gears of adaptational work. It creates markers around which a group of people can coordinate their activities. The task of converting anguished calls-of-distress into problem-solving work is further facilitated at reception by professional helpers who arrange at each contact for the subsequent contact. The adaptational pace is cemented by a set of scheduled convenings. Conversely, reception practices which do not yield a plan and schedule tend to suppress the level of active application to the work of solving problems. When one is "coming apart at the seams," it is energizing to arrive in a place where the people learn the burden of one's troubles, but then, without diffidence, seek to set purposes and pace. A format which socially regulates the pace seems to generate the decision, "Now is the time to get on with my work." "This is the place to do it." "I want to get started."

A word should be said about the strategy of offering a definite schedule in the face of "incomplete information." The workers at reception never have complete information. They seldom can be sure "it's going to work." But the basal purpose is to begin the suspended work of the adaptational interval within the fleeting period of its expression. And the fact is, plans can always change. Purpose and pace can be redefined and often are. Seldom is anything lost by setting dates and allocating responsibilities. Getting started yields a momentum which changes the context of all that follows.

If the professional helpers demonstrate an attractive style for pacing adaptational work, families pick it up. Then there is a network of allies. Families also appear to notice when a staff does not carry peculiar ideologic burdens. They take notice when their technical helpers are not looking for scapegoats: for example, "schizophrenogenic mothers" or "depriving husbands." If the staff is saying, "We'll hold this conference at a time when you can come. We can meet Tuesday evening," the family will hear they are being called to duty. They detect when they are in a situation in which they will be expected to make a contribution intrinsic to the outcome. They can hear "please." They can get excited about meaningful work.

SYSTEM CHANGES RESULTING FROM RECEPTION SERVICE

The clinical consequences in the life of a particular individual that result from entry into care by means of a systematic reception service, appear to be constructive out of all proportion to the cost. And the consequences are the most dramatic in situations where the individual's troubles are the most profound. The greater the extent to which chronic disability and social isolation intrude into the picture, the more striking is the impact of contact with a systematic package of services arranged at reception. Everyone needs a social network to perform the regulatory actions during the adaptational interval. But a socially isolated person is more likely to achieve contact with one if he enters service through systematic, modern reception. Everyone can benefit from prompt entry into pending adaptational work at crisis, but the individual with chronic disability is more likely to do so via systematic reception. For many individuals, reception service increases the likelihood of receiving the right service at the right time.

Because reception activities tend to enlarge the effects of assistance given to many of those who pass through other services, such work tends to take on additional kinds of yield. Reception practices come to exercise a systematic impact on the design of local services. The residents of the settlement soon use less inpatient service and more outpatient service. Experience from many centers, but particularly San Francisco,[32-36] Rockford, Illinois,[37] and Dutchess County, New York[38], establishes with uncommon confidence that fewer persons will use inpatient care, and for shorter intervals, after a pattern of systematic reception practices is introduced to a particular settlement, Part of this reduced use of inpatient care results from successful service in outpatient care[39], daycare[40], and home care[41] of persons apparently bound for inpatient settings, but deflected at reception to more precise varieties of care. Another part of the reduction results from the fact that seriously ill individuals may previously have been routed directly to a hospital, when no other general reception service was available. And most of the individuals so routed received a service emphasizing care in the same hospital where they were assessed on first contact.

Reception activity sometimes results in salutary changes in the scale of cooperative relationships among the agencies of a particular area. The staffs can develop an increased knowledge of each others' practices through their participation in multi-agency formats of reception. Such agencies tend to accelerate the volume of their joint programming, and frequently move toward a format for the clinical record which is standardized to allow more cooperation.[42] A type of inter-agency service agreement providing "packages" of service, the symmetrical, non-decline service agreement, can develop.[42] In such an agreement, each of two or more agencies which has been taking care of some of the same people in the same settlement agree to service all referrals from each other. Perhaps one agency has been serving adult male alcoholics on the east side of town, while another has been serving those on the west side of town. Perhaps one agency services referrals by physicians, while the other receives from welfare agencies. Agencies which discover a shared category of clientele agree to assess individuals on behalf of the services of their combined capacity. "You refer to me and I'll accept all you refer." "I will refer to you and you will accept all I refer." "Then we will get together periodically and talk about any imprecision in our referral habits."

Such agreements have the consequence of transferring difficulties in entering the service system from the circumstances of the patient-at-the-door-in-the-night to an inter-agency administrative conference, from negotiation by the patient to negotiation among professionals. Such agreements also make distinctly more productive use of the staff hours spent in assessment at reception.

A reception service often becomes a focus of civic interest. It offers an attractive spot for citizens to express their concerns about local mental health services. As a reception facility comes to function as a principal point of entrance into many local services, it develops an increasingly more general linkage with the goal aspirations of the citizens of that community. The citizens come to exercise a closer, more confident scrutiny of the practices of the facility. For example, they may seek to assure that an individual's rights and values are protected as he moves into services. Citizens sometimes decide that an ombudsman-like activity is intrinsic to work of reception. They often indicate an interest in insuring that the style and values expressed in the operations of the facility remain generally congruous with local sentiments.

The citizens regularly decide to ask the reception staff to attempt to receive each and every person who presents for service, the so-called "non-decline principle," and to service all persons only in local facilities cooperating in joint-programming activity, "the non-export principle." The effects of the non-decline and non-export principles, and the citizen interest in efforts to implement such objectives, tend to draw many types of local services increasingly into a system. Citizen activity to examine the practices and events at reception tends to make a hitherto unavailable category of information available to them. The availability of information developed in connection with a reception facility constitutes a new view of the settlement, a "closing of the feedback loop." Residents can learn about which roles and situations are most likely to result in trouble severe enough to warrant presentation to the reception point. And they are offered another basis upon which to consider changes in their patterns of service and patterns of living.

SUMMARY

Reception service is a place where resources can come into contact with persons-in-distress and become services. Because reception occurs at the earliest point in service, it offers the special opportunity to originate the right group of services for an individual's situation, and to pace service so as to use the flexibility of the adaptational interval. Altogether surprising changes are resulting from the introduction of reception services, perhaps because no other service setting can as well open the person and the system to self-discovery. Modern reception practices are allowing many to reaffirm the ancient observation that the satisfactions of adaptational accomplishment may last longer than the relief of sanctuary.

VI

UPDATED DESIGNS
FOR SERVICE

Services that aim to assist individuals in resuming temporarily suspended adaptational work are developing rapidly over wide areas of the United States. The discoveries that are emerging through such activities make this one of the most active areas in contemporary psychiatry. The rate of new developments in these fields is so brisk, that it may still be too early to formulate a stable theory concerning designs for local service. Some surprises and reformulations may lie ahead.

Although local services show considerable variation and experimentation, many workers appear to be concentrating on a relatively few trends. Several of these trends have grown out of efforts, which have in recent years grown more numerous, to relate much of psychiatric practice to the ordinary mechanics of adaptational work:

The timing of an individual's entrance to service is moving closer to the onset of symptoms, or to the collapse of the social network.

The site of reception into service and the site of the main service activities are moving closer to the individual's usual space of life.

The persons engaged in the service activities, in assessing the trouble and in evaluating the treatment plan, are growing in number. More attempts are being made to include as many persons, from both the network and service systems, as can make an efficient contribution. Much human adaptational work seems to require the participation of a social surround, provision for which emerges as a basic element of service design.

The objectives of service are becoming more explicit. The helpers are endeavoring to specify the nature of the pending adaptational work or the disability that requires amelioration. *Changes* in these same specifics define the *product* of service, and represent the standards within which the effectiveness of service is reckoned.

The behavior and operations comprising the service activities of staff personnel show a sharper outline than formerly. *Special effort is given to ascertaining which activities are essential to the intended design for service.* What do the service agents do that enhances the client's adaptational work? As such "active principles" become known, the service agents redefine the composition of their activities.

The duration of service encounters is shortening as service designs become more precise. Local service personnel show a keen interest in disencumbering their activity from unnecessary amounts of continuing contact and from other recruitatory practices.

Criteria defining the proper occasion of exit from service are growing more prominent in definitions of service design. Frequently, a set of behaviors or events which will signal that the objectives of service have been attained is defined early in service, so its appearance later can be recognized easily.

It is hard to escape the prominence in these trends of an awareness of the biology of the adaptational interval. Also showing a strong profile, is an interest which everywhere focuses on a set of observable events, rather than on hard-to-confirm practitioners' impressions.

Because the design trends described above appear to exert a major impact on the consequences of service, the terms which refer to them have become a standard vocabulary for discussing key features of a service plan. Descriptions of the timing, setting, participants, objectives, activities, duration and exit criteria appear prominently in contemporary efforts to represent a design briefly. Therefore, in the balance of this discussion, the term "service design" refers to such factors in a service contact or program as are thought to be responsible for whatever are its regularly predictable consequences. Service specifications may be discussed as they relate to a diffuse clientele, such as "designs for elderly persons," or to a narrower grouping, such as "designs for adult, socially isolated, chronic schizophrenic persons." In either sense, the evolving language of service design appears to offer a helpful advance in the ability to compare several possible plans for serving a particular cluster of problems. Recent interest in a more satisfactory language for service design also coincides with the appearance of services increasingly differentiated by problem or purpose.

The definition of the term "service" which is at the base of this inquiry describes an event, and its connection with a set of desired consequences: *Service is an encounter comprising purposefully arranged activities that occupy a short part of a life cycle, and that result in persisting increases in adaptational capacity, particularly capacities which continue beyond the cessation of contact.*

Note, in Diagram 3, that the service event is relatively much shorter than the life interval portrayed, and also shorter than the duration of the depicted consequences (an increase in adaptational capacity). In a particular case, this might mean, for example, that a four-month episode of service for a destructively heavy user of alcohol resulted in a situation of gainful employment and near-abstinence which lasted for a period of 17 months. Note also that when this

Diagram 3
A SERVICE EVENT DEFINED AS A RELATION BETWEEN
A BRIEF CONTACT AND PERSISTING CONSEQUENCES

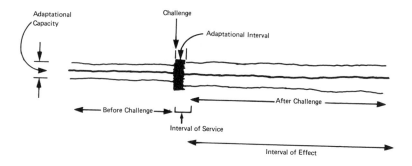

definition of service is applied to a condition of presumably life-long or extended risk, such as schizophrenia or some depressions, it results in a sequence of related service episodes, each with interspersed intervals of effect. A person might receive a phenothiazine medication continuously over decades, punctuated with periodic monitoring of the medication's effects. There might be, in addition, episodic assistance in handling current life problems. Diagram 4 depicts a series of service events, each with effects that persist for a limited period of time only. Whether one is considering a single event of service for a temporary condition, or a series of service events for a continuing risk, one aspect of the human value of the service inheres in the consequences that endure beyond the interval of the service contact. The professionals conducting many current service projects show a much greater interest than formerly was standard in learning which of the activities transpiring during the interval of contact are the ones that control the yield of a persisting situation of improvement. Although this category of curiosity is still unfolding, a few examples of what has already been discovered can illustrate the promise in such inquiry. Particularly promising are discoveries relating to social designs enhancing residential services, convening practices

Diagram 4
A Series of Service Events for a
Persisting Life Condition of Risk

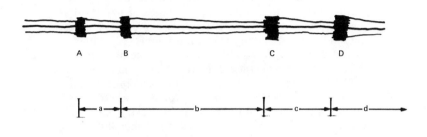

A,B,C,D = Service events
a, b, c, d = Effects persisting beyond the service
event but not indefinitely

in outpatient (nonresidential) services, and designs which make services for prolonged or life-long conditions helpful without being toxic.

RESIDENTIAL CARE AS A PLACE THAT HEALS

In the 1840s, when Dorothea Dix traveled across America, she carried a two-part message. America's mentally ill were being mistreated. And they were being mistreated because they were in the wrong kind of place, in prisons[1]:

> About two years since leisure afforded opportunity and duty prompted me to visit several prisons and almshouses in the vicinity of this metropolis [Boston], I found, near Boston, in the jails and asylums for the poor, a numerous class brought into unsuitable connection with criminals and the general mass of paupers. I refer to idiots and insane persons, dwelling in circumstances not only adverse to their own physical and moral improvement, but productive of extreme disadvantages to all other persons brought into association with them . . . . Prisons are not constructed in view of being converted

into county hospitals, and almshouses are not founded as receptacles for the insane. And yet, in the face of justice and common sense, wardens by law are compelled to receive and the masters of almshouses not to refuse, insane and idiotic subjects in all stages of mental disease and privation . . . . [I] could give many examples. Let one suffice. A young woman, a pauper, in a distant town, Sandisfield, was for years a raging maniac. A cage, chains, and the whip were the agents for controlling her, united with harsh tones and profane language. Annually, with others, the town's poor, she was put up at auction, and bid off at the lowest price which was declared for her . . . . I proceed, gentlemen, briefly to call your attention to the present state of insane persons confined within this Commonwealth, in cages, closets, cellars, stalls, and pens! Chained, naked, beaten with rods, and lashed into obedience.

And Miss Dix had a remedy in mind, which she proposed in the form of an illustrative case review[1]:

She had set at defiance all efforts for controlling the contaminating violence of her excited passions. Every variety of blasphemous expression, every form of polluting phraseology, was poured forth in torrents, sweeping away every decent thought, and giving reality to that blackness of darkness which, it is said, might convert a heaven into a hell. There, day after day, month after month . . . . The *law* permitted her there, and there she remained till July last, when, after an application to the judge [in a manner] so determined that all refusal was refused, a warrant was granted for her transfer to the State Hospital. I saw her there two weeks since. What a change! Decent, orderly, neatly dressed, capable of light employment, partaking with others her daily meals . . . . Not a rational woman by any means, but no longer a nuisance . . . . she exhibited how much could be done for the most unsettled and apparently the most hopeless cases by being placed in a situation adapted to the wants and necessities of her condition. Transformed from a very Tisiphone, she is now a controllable woman.

But this most wonderful change may not be lasting. She is liable to be returned to the prison, as have been others, and then no question but in a short time like scenes will distract and torment all in a vicinity so much to be dreaded.

A particular notion blossomed from the social concepts of the time[2/3]. The notion held that a place termed a "hospital," properly situated in the country, and arranged down to the last detail to achieve a benign style of life, could exert a healing effect. It was a time of building orphan asylums, reformatories, penitentiaries and mental hospitals. The tenor of the times resonated with scientific findings and theoretical formulations that focused professional interest on attempts to heal by altering the environment. And the alteration of the environment that was most frequently undertaken had to do with removing an individual from an ordinary environment, and placing him in special, micro-utopian environments termed asylums. The belief that a proper social environment could, first, be defined, and then could be applied to certain ills, had its origins in the nineteenth-century concept that civilization was the controlling factor in explaining human experience. If health and competence are a function of enculturation, then so too are sickness and poverty. Though man was clearly the product of imperfect societies and imperfect governments, such communities and governments were seen to have the capacity for change and reform. It was quite natural, since both health and illness appeared to have a social etiology, that treatment methods would involve the creation of a type of society, "the moral treatment." It was also natural that there might evolve an institutional setting under a type of government, a psychiatric mode of administration, with its own guild and technology[2].

Consider Kirkbride's notion concerning the restorative power of a properly equipped bucolic paradise[4]:

The pleasure grounds and farm of the Pennsylvania Hospital for the Insane, comprise a tract of one hundred and ten acres of well improved land, lying two miles west of the City of Philadelphia, between the Westchester and Haverford roads, on the latter of which is the only gate of entrance. Of this land, forty-one and three-quarter acres constitute the pleasure grounds which surround the Hospital buildings and are enclosed by a substantial stone wall, of an average height of ten and a half feet. The remaining sixty-nine and one-quarter acres comprise the farm of the Institution. From the character of the ground near the Hospital, the wall surrounding the pleasure grounds is so arranged as to be almost entirely out of sight from the buildings, and only a small part of it can be seen from any one point within the enclosure . . . .

The deer-park is specially appropriated to the use of the male patients. In this division is a fine grove of large trees, several detached clumps of various kinds, and a great variety of single trees standing alone or in avenues along the different walks, which, of brick, gravel or tan, are for the men, more than a mile and a quarter in extent. The groves are fitted with seats and summer houses, and have various means of exercise and amusement connected with them.

There is a single private yard of good size for gentlemen who wish to be less public than in the grounds, or for those whose mental condition renders more seclusion desirable. The yard is planted with trees and has broad brick walks passing round it. Between the north lodge and the deer park, separated from the latter by a sunken palisade fence, is a neat flower garden. In connection with each lodge are three small yards paved with brick and accessible to the patients of the respective divisions with which they are connected. The work shop and lumberyard are just within the main entrance on the west—adjoining which is a fine grove, in which is a gentlemen's ten-pin alley.

In the pleasure grounds of the ladies, is a fine piece of woods, from which the farm is overlooked, as well as both of the public roads passing along the premises, and a handsome district of country beyond. The wall here is forty feet below the platform on which the Hospital stands, and is at the foot of a steep hill, so that it is not seen at all unless persons are in its immediate proximity.

The summer-houses, rustic-seats, exercising-swings, etc., in this division, are all in particularly pleasant positions. The cottage fronts the woods, and in every part this portion of the grounds is completely protected from intrusion and observation.

The undulating character of the pleasure grounds throughout, gives them many advantages, and the brick, gravel and tan walks for the ladies, are more than a mile in extent . . . .

In the arrangement and location of the walks for the patients, great pains have been taken to give as much extent and variety as possible, and to bring into view objects of interest, not only within the enclosure, but in the well improved district of country immediately around the Hospital.

The carriage road is sufficiently extended to give a pretty thorough view of the whole grounds, and of the farm and scenery beyond. This is occasionally used very advantageously for giving carriage exercise to patients who could not with propriety be taken to more public situations.

The fences that have been put up, were rendered necessary by the users to which the different parts of the grounds were appropriated. A large part of palisade fences, like those enclosing the deer park and drying-yard, were to effect the separation of the sexes, and the close fences have been made, almost invariably, for the sole purpose of protecting the patients from observation, and giving them the proper degree of privacy . . . .

From this account one can appreciate the detail of preparation entailed in arranging such a very specific character of environment. This "asylum" is separated from ordinary life and affairs, orderly within a utopian concept of rectitude and governed by a wise elite. The combined notions of government, benign social order and confined population are sufficiently prominent in these arrangements to project a picture of a moral-political enterprise directed to the formation of a colony.

Contemporary spokesmen held confident views of the impact this plan of care would have[5]:

> The cost of curing a case of insanity in a good hospital, and returning the patient to his family and to usefulness in society, is not, on the average, one-tenth of what it is to support a chronic uncared case for life. This is the economical point of view, in regard to making adequate provision for the prompt and enlightened treatment of all the insane of every class and description, even if no account is made of the value of restoring to usefulness in a community, one of its producing members . . . .

Several elements of the construction and equipage of the hospital buildings illustrate the importance attached to arranging for a stable social order[5]:

> The buildings should be in a healthful, pleasant, and fertile district of country. The land chosen should be of good quality and easily tilled. The surrounding scenery should be varied and attractive. The neighborhood should possess numerous objects of an agreeable and interesting character. While the hospital itself should be retired, and its privacy fully secured, the views from it, if possible, should exhibit life in its active forms, and on this account stirring objects at a little distance are desirable . . . .
>
> The arrangement [of buildings ought to] permit the division of excited patients into very small companies. The mingling of large numbers of this class [is] very subversive to good order and often detrimental to individual patients, especially when the cases are recent.
>
> The most satisfactory [arrangement] provides for the accommodation of sixteen distinct classes of male patients. Each one of the sixteen wards [should comprise], besides the corridors for promenading, and the chambers of the patients and attendants, a parlor, a dining-room, a bath-room, a water-closet, a sink-room, a

wash-room, a drying-closet, a storeroom, a clothes-room, a dumb-waiter, a dust-flue, and a stairway by which persons can pass out of doors or to the center building, as may be desired, without communication with the other wards . . . .

Even when thus proportioned, two hundred and fifty [persons] will be found about as many as the medical superintendent can visit properly every day, or nearly every day, in addition to the performance of his other duties . . . .

The locks in a hospital for the insane are subjected to such constant use that they should be made with great care. The parts most likely to wear should be case-hardened. The keys for the male and female wards should be so entirely different that it will be impossible by any slight alteration to make those for one side open the locks for the other . . . .

It is desirable that the pleasure-grounds and garden should be securely enclosed, to protect the patients from the gaze and impertinent curiosity of visitors, and from the excitement occasioned by their presence in the grounds . . . .

A view of the certitude surrounding the provisions for the design and governance of this healing space emerges from a contemporary discussion within a professional society[6]:

No Hospital for the Insane should be built, without the plan having been first submitted to some physician or physicians who have had charge of a similiar establish-ment or are practically acquainted with all the details of their arrangements, and received his or their full ap-probation . . . .

The ability to govern such an environment was some-times thought to arise from medical training[7]:

The medical superintendent, whatever he may wish to be [termed], is essentially an executive officer. If he is deficient in practical ability, though he might write a volume on the cerebral anatomy of a spider . . . [he] would be of no value whatever. His specialty is insane-hospital management. From force of circumstances he comes to know the insane as a mother knows her children. [He] gains a knowledge of them which no one can get who does not live with them . . . . There is something in the training of the medical man which makes him a little different from what he would otherwise be, for he is more gentle, tolerant, patient, appreciative, and sympathetic in dealing with poor human nature. Call the medical superintendent "farmer," "steward," "caterer," "treasurer," or whatsoever name we choose, there still beats within his breast a heart not dead to the cry of suffering and distress . . . .

Residential concepts of service were so dominant in the nineteenth century, as to constitute an almost unanimous ratification of a single design for service. This unanimity of approach did not derive so much from scientifically secure observations concerning their effectiveness, as from the personal convictions of a few pioneers. These early workers moved with apparent confidence from a small base of clinical observations toward an advocacy, with political resonances, of a new public-policy[2]. Eventually, the prominence of asylum-style notions of treatment began to decline; the unraveling of the factors behind the decline has proved an exciting detective story for historians[2]. The central clinical observation is that life in asylum is not a reliable method of healing the mentally ill. The method proved less effective and more costly than would allow for it to remain in a position of continuing dominance. Further, its decline from dominance was made possible by the appearance of methods which worked better.

RESIDENTIAL CARE AS A STARTING PLACE FOR DISCOVERY

In order to follow the systems that evolved out of the residential service characteristic of the mid-nineteenth century, we can summarize the asylum method using the more recent language of service design. Studies of the method's *timing, setting, participants, objectives, activities, duration* and *end point*, have influenced practioners to restrict the use of the residential approach to an ever-narrowing group of people. And the end of such restriction is not yet in sight. Several recent major leaps away from the asylum concept illustrate the way in which a service strategy grounded in science eventually works its way to dominance over an original, plausible, shot-in-the-dark. Note that the asylum model emphasizes a separated, simplified social space which would work its way by virtue of how different it was from ordinary environments. It was thought that the daily activities and social contacts of the residents would influence their return to health precisely because such elaborate care was taken to radically disconnect them from more ordinary situations.

Now, however, one of the strongest trends in more recent residential service design erases the effort to create "separate" settings and social contacts (See table 4 for a scheme of the contrast). And twentieth-century professionals visualize much mental illness and symptoms as the interaction of physiologic and situational factors which fix and prolong adaptational behavior. Consequently, they expect to relieve symptoms primarily by activities which enhance the performance of pending adaptational work (see Chapter III). Therefore, recent residential service designs tend to hang on efforts to restart aborted adaptation, and, necessarily, to situate such work in settings offering an opportunity to test its products. Consequently, residential service settings tend increasingly to resemble ordinary circumstances, and to be peopled with individuals temporarily drawn in from those same ordinary circumstances. Into such settings is drawn a blend of temporary task-groups made up of members of patients' families and friends, together with other patients and a few professionals.

The movement toward brief, task-focused residential care has grown out of a series of observations, many of which might have surprised the inventors of asylum. Several of these observations relate to basic functions of the social

Table 4
RESIDENTIAL SERVICE TRENDS OVER THE PAST CENTURY

Design Component	Nineteenth-Century Asylum Concept	Mid-Twentieth-Century Residential Concepts
Timing	Last resort	Early, easy entrance
Setting	Rural, enclosed, utopian social order	Local, open, small, ordinary
Participants	Superintending staff, excluding family and neighbors	Staff, other patients, family, friends, neighbors
Objectives	Return to general health prior to release from setting	Stabilization only of physiological aspects as a brief phase of other service
		Some prolonged use as a life setting for a still-declining number of persons
Activities	Colonial work and recreation	Focused task-work, medical service, first steps of a problem-solving sequence
Duration	Indefinite	Days to weeks
Endpoint	Cessation of condition of insanity	Commencement of problem-solving activity, physiologic stability, resumption of ordinary role activity

context, functions like regulating the onset, pacing, focus and cessation of adaptational work (see Chapter III). Other observations relate to the choice of the setting for such work, particularly as to whether it can provide opportunities to survey a current life problem or to test promising responses to that problem. Whereas the asylum creators believed that unique settings and social networks were advantageous, many of the subsequent observations testify to the greater usefulness of more ordinary settings and networks.

Take, for example, the notion of governance of the social order within the hospital or residential setting. The nineteenth-century concept envisioned two separated groupings of people, one of staff, one of patients, with an interface based on compliance and benevolence. Twentieth-century observers gradually detected the fact that faster return to ordinary life occurred when patients were expected to form or participate in certain governance groupings within the treatment setting, and to undertake other cooperative actions. Many of these groupings and actions softened or broke away the earlier two-group interface and replaced the prior compliance-benevolence relations[8]. Observations of the behavior of staff, and of patients, especially in institutions where the average duration of residence is measured in months or years, tended to demonstrate that most persons, whether of staff or patient status, act as if they are part of one and the same social system. For instance, instances of fighting activity by patients, of kinds which transgress local conduct norms, were found to occur in close timing with instances of fighting activity by staff, activity which also transgresses local patterns for making decisions[9]. Another line of observation testified to the fact that service styles that confine an individual to the same setting and social system for the whole of a twenty-four hour day, tend to destroy many of the very same social skills the service intends to enhance[10]. The notion has gradually dawned on many that the decision to create a separated social order, based on colonial hierarchy and governance, probably arose as a service design rather than from factors intrinsic to most types of mental illness. For example, the removal of the locks that formerly secured residential settings has resulted in fewer, rather than more "escapes"[11]. Also, when the professional staff allowed it, rather than interfering with it, patients were found to spontaneously form small social groups and establish practices to assist each other in the conduct of adaptational work[12]. When staff broke up these groups, exacerbation of symptoms ensued together with increased transgression of local norms of conduct[12].

Many twentieth-century studies have tended to confirm the observation that individuals serviced in residential settings conduct a category of adaptational work which equips them suitably for continued institutional life, but just as surely eclipses other skills required for ordinary life settings[10]. The more prolonged is the period of residential service[13-16], and the more complete the twenty-four hour enclosure[10,17/18], the more profound is the ablation of patterns necessary for life in ordinary settings. Other observations suggest that service in a residential setting may confer an increased risk of suicide during the first several months following discharge from such a setting, a risk beyond that for the age and condition[19].

On the other hand, several classes of observations demonstrate that residential service can be freed of many of the problems deriving from the original asylum style. Once loosened from their former extraneous encumbrances, residential settings can move into previously unsuspected levels of effectiveness. For example, when the scale of a mental hospital residential unit is small, perhaps under 20 persons, a much more rapid movement through the setting toward ordinary locations occurs than with larger units [20/21]. Also, when the staff of such a unit concentrates its energies on detecting and reacting to any display of competent behavior, the rate of return to ordinary settings shows distinct increases[21]. Another line of observation shows that mental-health professionals in large residential service settings frequently seem to have an easier time detecting incompetent behavior, than in noticing reasonable, problem-solving activity[22-24]. Related studies also show that if the staff shifts the focus of their attention away from detecting deranged behavior, and toward exquisite vigilance for more conventional behavior, patients blossom with a dramatically enhanced performance[25-28].

Any residential service exists in a field of other local services and other elements of local civic experience. Many mid-twentieth-century explorations in residential service design have a tendency to connect what goes on inside the residential setting with what goes on outside. Each of a wide range of such inside-outside connections seems to increase the rate of movement through the facility, and yield an earlier return to more ordinary locations. For example, increasing the amount of visiting activity has such an effect[28]. Similar effects are observed when the residential setting is set up to direct its services to the residents of a particular settlement, and when the general citizenry of that area acquires a role in the development of its operating policies[29-34].

Several of these trends in the design of residential service operate so as to move it from asylum to interlude, from sanctuary to workshop. Diagram 5 summarizes the changing relation of residential services to a local social context. Note that, at the "asylum" stage, troubled people are attracted into a distant, enclosed place of service; but that as increasing numbers arrive, the effect of service is increasingly diluted and colonial. In the "temporary network" stage, individuals move "through" the service, making contact with helpful people and programs, and then return to more ordinary environments. In the "linkage-assist" model, individuals make contact with several services, including some placed in residential circumstances, but all the while retain or renew a set of vital linkages with their ordinary networks and environments. The asylum model lends itself to study as an almost-closed vessel; the temporary network resembles a pipeline; the linkage-assist, a conducted tour of a local shopping center. The capacity of the first is related to the scale of the social unit, that of the second to the velocity or transit time in the service, that of the third to the precision of the linkages made.

As residential settings increasingly become the setting for only a limited phase of quite variable designs for care,

Diagram 5
EVOLUTION OF THE CONCEPT OF RESIDENTIAL SERVICE

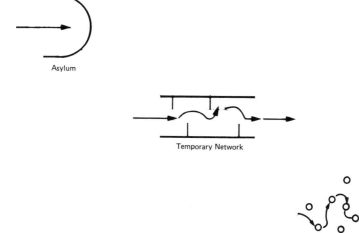

Asylum

Temporary Network

Linkage-Assist

their original design is sprouting in several directions. For instance, hospital-like activities are prominent, as in the treatment of health problems affecting behavior and the nervous system, or the stabilization of biochemical components of schizophrenia and depression. Schoolroom activities flourish almost as much, as for example, exchange of information, searching a problem and testing opinions. Parlor-like activities, such as family decision-making and reconciliation, are salient in the mix. But, because residential services tend to be more costly than other types, many practitioners are attempting to unravel a view of what is best done in residential settings. Almost every kind of service has, at one time or another, been conducted in residential settings. And almost every component of an array of services has been tried in non-residential locations.

Where such sifting and sorting will go, it is yet too early

to say. Several observations appear warranted. Residential settings have clear advantages whenever physical control or observation for more than several hours is essential. Residential settings—for example, hospitals—offer overwhelming advantages whenever intense medical or physiological service is needed. And they appear to serve beneficially whenever twenty-hour, reliable supervision or human surveillance is needed. Some of the problems which require such conditions include situations like withdrawal from a narcotic or addicting substance, stabilization of a physiologic abnormality, provision of a temporary social system to a totally isolated person, protection of individuals from acutely lethal behavior, and holding, while observing, an individual whose situation cannot be ascertained quickly.

But because a whole new productivity is transforming the purposes and methods of residential service, the story is just beginning. Much of the rest of the evolution will necessarily call for observations of residential service as a part of a care system within a larger array of options. Since it has been established that residential service cannot encompass the whole, the way is clearer to select it for the parts wherein it excels.

Guideline 10: The more closely a residential service resembles an individual's usual circumstances of living, the more pertinent will be the adaptational work there conducted.

Guideline 11: Most of the technical activities which warrant the use of residential service can be conducted in such a manner as to enhance an individual's connectedness with the people and adaptational challenges in his ordinary life.

Guideline 12: When an individual is in need of domicile, as well as other service, it is ordinarily advantageous to supply such added service in extra-domiciliary settings. Conversely, extended services-in-domicile, especially collective domicile, acquire a momentum toward asylum.

Guideline 13: Adaptational work conducted in a controlled or tailored residential environment, including ones designed for health service, tends to be of such a type as to develop a continuing need for the persistence of such an environment.

Guildeine 14: The people who conduct the technical work in a residential setting can tend to dominate most of the currently active attachment activity of an individual while in service, and, thereby, eclipse the prior connections to a more enduring, ordinary network. Measures which assure daily contact with people from the context of more usual associations act to prevent such eclipsing effects.

UPDATING THE REST OF SERVICES

COHORTING SOCIAL ISOLATES   In earlier chapters we outlined the intrinsic role the social context plays in relation to success-ful adaptational work. Much of the recent activity in design-ing services consists of exploring ways either to provide temporary task-groups for isolated people, or ways to con-vene the fragmenting networks of those who are not so iso-lated. Arranging for such a social surround, whether tempo-rary or ordinary, appears to place a set of semi-automatic actions into operation; these actions tend to "regulate" a per-son's work, advancing him from efforts to describe his trou-bles, toward efforts to decide on a course and take action. Surprisingly, these regulatory functions may be carried on by any one of several types of small clusters of people. The cluster may be comprised of kin, or friends, or of persons in a religious or situational affiliation. It may be an *ad hoc* mutual-help group, or, quite often, a set of persons who happen to be passing through the agency at the same time.

In an earlier day, professionals sometimes provided themselves as the social substrate for adaptational work, often terming it "a personal relationship." The tradition in which a person termed a "therapist" assists an individual to figure out who he is, where he is going and what problems obstruct the way is old and well-traveled. Although trying to conduct problem-solving work in social isolation has serious limitations[35-39], other hazards lurk in the approach which tries to correct such isolation by arranging social encounters with professionals. This path has been shown to create a category of solution dependent upon continuing contact with professionals. And problem-solving work regulated mainly by professionals results in highly resilient links between formerly serviced clients and those same professionals. The convoluted elasticity of those crisis-wrought links in the face of later "discharge" efforts has proved considerable. Many of such links remain active well beyond the interval of the crisis and provide a momentum toward continuing patienthood.

Consequently, many current designs for service are moving toward practices which convene and assemble, rather than supply and replace. Practices which draw together members of a persisting social network for focused task-work are termed "convening." Practices which draw together isolated persons, or individuals with no prior associations, are called "cohorting." Observations show that such convening and cohorting are so effective that they may become a major component of services[27,40-45].

Convening is made possible by the fact that a crisis generally causes a social network to temporarily increase its potential for realignments. The possibility for cohorting derives from similar increases in affiliational behavior on the part of isolated persons as they pass through the adaptational state, combined with the opportune fact that a cluster of such persons is often in service at the same time. Although there are relatively few isolated persons in a given area—

they generally comprise less than five percent of the overall population[46]—the cohorting option exists because they do, in most cases, represent a much larger fraction of the "service" population; and even a majority among those engaged in repeating or prolonged service patterns[35/36]. Diagram 6 represents the gradual transition from isolation to temporary group affiliation, as the isolate passes through service. Note that professionals interested in cohorting isolated persons direct their primary affiliative effort toward enhancing the formation of social connections among a set of otherwise isolated clients. This path is chosen because the professionals know that, since they themselves will remain with the program, any clients who become attached to them will also tend to remain. On the other hand, sets of affiliations among clients, each of whom is moving through the service program, carry less of this recruitatory hazard. The phenomenon of cohorting results in clusters of clients who move through an episode of service and return to their ordinary life situation, having gained increased adaptational ability. Further, their improved situation is derived from active affiliations, but is not dependent upon continuing contact with service personnel.

Some of the cohorting groups last only for weeks, whereas others persist for several years. The value of even

Diagram 6
COHORTING ISOLATES DURING TRANSIT IN SERVICE

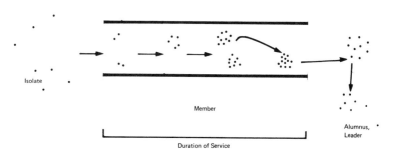

Isolate

Member

Alumnus,
Leader

Duration of Service

temporary groups to isolated persons resides in the fact that they encourage a more effective variety of adaptational work, as well as in the fact that the isolate's often-atrophied affiliational skills become reactivated, and often persist beyond the service interval. More often than not, the temporary task-groups act as bridges to more persisting affiliations, rather than as enduring social units.

The actual nature of the activities such cohorts conduct exerts less effect on the service result than does the presence of an attractive format of roles, conventions and projects. For example, although the members of groups engaged in some set of activities envisioned to lead toward a complicated goal such as "insight" into their behavior, can develop roles and projects which might sustain their continuing affiliation, more often, the fact that the professional must by definition assume a major role in psychotherapy, impedes the formation of any pattern of linkages that would be independent of him. Linkages that are not dependent upon professionals[12], or upon efforts to gain intellectual understanding of what is happening[47-49] offer the most resilience during adaptational stresses. An approach that is typical of current cohorting methods simply draws a set of persons known to be isolated into a room, and asks them to get ready to undertake a project they find interesting in a way they find enjoyable[50-51]. The range of projects these groups pursue, even during their formative period in service, is large. Brief activities like making a spaghetti dinner for the clients and staff of an agency can energize such a group to get organized. Longer and more complex activities, such as making instructional materials for helping pre-school children learn to read, can lead to more enduring affiliations. Less important than the specifics of the project, is that it yield a product whose value is clear to all, and is distinctly worth the individual effort— especially the effort to set foot into the unfamiliar terrain of group affiliations. Less important than the exact pattern of organization is that it be one that includes all members of the cohort, but excludes the professional who convened them.

The professional, or "assistant to the group," is not,

properly speaking the "leader," because the role of leader is one proper to a member. The activities of such an assistant are critical, nevertheless, in any situation involving a cluster of isolates. The action he takes to draw isolated individuals together in a room, at an early point in their interval of service, creates an occasion otherwise absent. His calling on each individual present to speak about a skill he enjoys, sets the scene for that individual to move toward the group. If the group assistant asks the people assembled to consider carrying on a joint project, he gives them a convenient opportunity to create a pattern for making decisions, for conducting group business. If he asks that they "decide on the project by the weekend" so they "can gather their materials over the next week," he acts to pace and focus their energies. The group assistant enables the group to get going, fundamentally by regulating the pace while avoiding the acquisition of any role. For instance, when there is conflict, he asks "whether they are ahead or behind their schedule." When the activity of some few members takes center stage, thus eclipsing the entry possibilities of others, he asks "Whether a project interesting only to some will call for the full energies of any?" More detailed technical examination of cohorting methods is properly the subject of other works[50]. It has a place in this discussion only to highlight that cohorting is an expanding activity, one with a basic role in service designs for individuals who, because of isolation, do not otherwise gain lasting benefit from service.

Cohorting activities are prominent in several types of settings—residential, daycare, outpatient care, and shelter-care homes and lodges. The physical setting seems to set up no obstacles to effective cohorting, so long as the group can control the use of the space during the time they employ it. Cohorting fits in smoothly with many other components of service as, for instance, medical study, drug administration, counseling or job training.

The origin of an individual's social isolation—whether because he is aged or migrant, or because of drug addiction or alcohol, or because of schizophrenia or recurring depression—does not seem to affect the manner or utility of cohorting. But in most cases, cohorting must be combined with other, essential components of service. Cohorting activities, for example, often improve the results of phenothiazine treatment with schizophrenic persons, but make no less essential the phenothiazines themselves. However, with anyone whose situation, for whatever reason, includes isolation, the effects of cohorting are of such magnitude as to warrant a corresponding emphasis in the basics of service design.

FROM ENCLAVED FIEFDOMS TO A COMMERCE OF SERVICES The purpose of services is to increase personal adaptivity. Variations in particular aspects of service design—such as timing, setting, participants, activities, duration and end point—surely account for major differences in the success of particular services. However, there is a further aspect of service design that seems to warrant inclusion as a major component of service effectiveness; namely, the possibility of offering two or more kinds of service to a single individual, whether simultaneously or in sequence. In Chapter V, it was seen that many individuals-in-distress present a profile of disabilities that could be most effectively ameliorated through several categories of service including, for instance, phenothiazine medication, counseling, cohorting and training for employment. In many areas of the United States, however, each of these several services might be conducted under separated auspices.

Continuity of approach across separate administrative domains persists as an important clinical stumbling block, in spite of yeoman efforts by many. The phenomenon of small, separate services under different auspices arose, historically, because each service originated in an interest in a particular doctrine or clientele, or sometimes through specific religious or guild affiliations. The observation that packages of previously separated services offer advantages in their clinical effects is neither a new observation, nor one often disputed. Yet headway in freeing the service array from its cottage industry origins advances all too slowly in many localities. Because such packaging and continuity can offer large clinical advantages, there is consequently much interest in exploring whatever strategies might allow such combining to proceed. Is there an approach to drawing services together which does not lead to other risks, such as cumbersome size and advancing bureaucracy? Is it possible to maintain respect for several traditional concerns of democratic societies, as, for instance, the goals of minimal government and maximum citizen freedom? Because, although guild and domain interests have played their part in maintaining small, independent services, so too has a reluctance to centralize, to append to the state, to politicize, in order to gain continuity.

Perhaps there is another approach to continuity and packaging, one related more to the design of services than to mergers or loss of pluralism. Let us reflect on several of the changes in service which follow from participation in a reception service, as discussed in Chapter V. For example, agency staffs develop an increased use of each other's services out of understandings developed through participating in a jointly conducted client reception. Such understandings often result in inter-agency referral agreements and in standardized formats for recording clinical activity, formats which are negotiated among agencies for a greater usefulness in multi-agency service efforts[51]. Perhaps features of other forms of service can have similar effects on continuity, without depending upon additional centralization.

The striking fact that the differing functions of the several settings of care complement one another very sharply, portends an eventual situation of open commerce. What inpatient care does best is enhanced by what outpatient care does best. What counseling does best is enhanced by what cohorting does best. Table 5 illustrates typical functions and durations for several different service settings. Note that there is already a natural specialization of function. The interdependence which is implied in such a specialization will gradually drive the separated services in a particular locale toward increased exchange in an ecology of activities. Or-

Table 5
DIFFERENTIATION IN LOCAL SERVICE ELEMENTS

Element	Task	Activity	Duration
Reception	Entrance	Convening	Hours
Outpatient	Adaptation	Regulating	Months
Inpatient	Alterations in physiology	Medical service	Days
Transitional*	Assembling new network	Role-testing	Months
Daycare	Repairs to network	Cohorting	Weeks
Repeating**	Derecruitment	Packages of service	Years

* For example, a halfway house
** Repeating or prolonged service for heavy users

dinarily, the types of local service available to individuals within any given area will include the following: *reception service*, which provides access; *inpatient service* which provides controlled environment for residence; *daycare and nightcare* services, which provide a treatment-oriented social system for a part of each day, but expect the patient to spend another part of each day in an independent social system; *outpatient service*, which provides intermittent service to enhance adaptive capacity; *home-care service*, which provides service set in a person's place of residence and usually involves his family; *transitional or shelter-care service*, such as a halfway house or sheltered workshop, in which the individual moves freely about the community some portions of the day or week, perhaps holding employment, but in which the setting of his work or residence is specifically modified so as to reduce a disability state; *repeating services*, including *after-care and communal re-entry service,* which provide packages of service for heavy users or persons who have been institutionalized for a long time, or repeatingly, and are now preparing to resume movement about the general community.

Note that the very differences in the dominant activities conducted in each setting carry a functional dynamic toward interaction among those settings. For example the clinical advantages of daycare[18] seem to arise from the possibility of offering intense technical service during a part of each day, while allowing the patient to maintain his activities in another social system during another part of each day[51]. On the other hand, the advantages of inpatient care pertain in those conditions where intense medical service and twenty-four hour control are required, such as in the chemical regulation of schizophrenia or depression, or in withdrawal from an addicting substance. The very properties that form the advantage of inpatient care, namely the possibility of regulation during the whole of a twenty-four hour period, will eventually move it into linkage with a daycare setting so as to gain the latter's capability to re-establish movement between two social systems.

The differences between services that derive from specialization by type of client, also foreshadow the evolution of a similar, interdependent commerce. Table 6 summarizes several specializations of activity by type of client served. For instance, activities directed toward withdrawing a person from an addicting drug, or the regulation of phenothiazine intake for a schizophrenic, make demands for medical skills. On the other hand, the application of cohorting methods to social isolates calls for skills relating to the profession of social work. Yet the clinical circumstance often arises, for example, in which an isolated person is also schizophrenic. The interest each type of service has in expanding its effectiveness provides a compelling dynamic toward eventual interdependence.

Several other dynamics provide a push toward a more open commerce among the service types in any local area. To the degree that the citizens in an area ask their professionals not to remove people-in-trouble to another settlement for services, the so-called "non-export principle," to that extent will such services tend to associate to provide through interaction what they formerly provided through export. Now, and increasingly into the future, local service systems operate out of the goal that service activity will result in fewer persons becoming disabled, and that for shorter periods of time. Local service activity has become increasingly locked into such a trend by the fact that social expectations have defined as a goal that the overall service system should continually act to reduce the export of people from the ordinary spaces of life. The service activities, taken as a whole, are therefore constrained to evolve in such a manner that the locality they service will not export persons to another local-

Table 6
ACTIVITIES IN SERVICES SPECIALIZED BY TYPE OF CLIENT

Activities Conducted In All Services	Activities Emphasized by Type of Client			
	Isolates	Schizophrenics	Children	Addicted Persons
Regulation of setting, network, pacing	Cohorting	Phenothiazines Butyrophenones	Services en famille	Domiciliary
Convening, diverting, detecting, converting, task-focusing, etc.	Assistance in forming mutual-help groups	Life-long duration of service	Foster family	Cohorted conversion
Cohorting		Crisis inputs	Non-eclipsing services	Entry through criminal code
		Pedigree inquiry	School settings	

ity. This whole line of civic intention acts to draw the service elements and auspices increasingly away from their earlier fiefdoms.

The residents of many settlements are asking their professionals to simplify and accelerate the qualifying routines prior to service. Such increased access often draws in to service new and challenging categories of troubled persons. The presence of such novel categories acts to loosen any fixity to earlier styles of service. Several tasks have recently, for example, been added into the basic local service responsibilities. Consider, for instance, the expanded interest in serving persons addicted to narcotics and alcohol, children and old people, non-residential management of mental retardation and in precise professional assistance to self-help groups such as Recovery Incorporated, First Friends, Alcoholics Anonymous and Synanon. There is every reason to assume that this process of adding new risk groups, and of stretching and expanding service tasks, will continue. As previously underserviced categories of troubled persons enter the service spectrum, it may become increasingly important to be able to offer a broader range of types of clinical service.

The more differentiation that occurs, the greater is the interdependence between each type of service. In fact, it is becoming evident that the interrelatedness of each of the settings and auspices enhances the effect of each, and that any service engagement with underserviced risk groups enhances effectiveness with all risk groups. The greater the extent to which users ask their services to move beyond the provision of sanctuary, the greater will be the requisite interaction to assure the pertinent adaptational work. And, the greater the extent to which users ask their professionals to set aside those forms of activity which dull or neutralize the intrinsic signaling actions of distress—thereby avoiding so far as possible, for example, medicating anxiety in healthy people—to that extent will the resulting services move into a network of interaction which can be in contact with the adaptational activities thus released.

Guideline 15: If a socially isolated individual requires mental health service, measures which provide such service in a setting that includes other, cohorted isolates will likely draw the individual into the commencement of pending adaptational work.

Guideline 16: The decision to provide an individual's pending service in such a setting as can permit both technical, professional action and contextual regulation of his adaptational work, ordinarily precedes all other decisions except those effecting the preservation of life.

LONG SERVICE FREED FROM TOXIC WRAPPINGS   Much of the discussion thus far assumes the time frame of an ordinary adaptational interval; that is, a period lasting from several weeks to several months. For instance, reception services focus on igniting a prompt initiation of adaptational work (see Chapter V). Residential and daycare services are conducted so as to furnish certain technical interventions, while at the same time they provide for the social context that regulates the behavior of the interval (see above). So long as the proper service for a given circumstance approximates in duration the length of a single adaptational episode, the biology of the adaptational state provides a reasonable analytic frame. Decisions regarding the timing, setting, participants, objectives, activities and endpoint can be reckoned out of the general strategy which aims to create the biological and social requisites for a successful episode of adaptation.

But an entirely different analytic framework enters whenever the expected length of the service interval greatly exceeds the measure of a single adaptational episode. Consider, for example, services for the schizophrenic. He carries a life-long biochemical disorder, a reduction in the kinetics of the catecholamines, one that predisposes him to faulty adaptational work; adaptational difficulties that are expressed in a series of life challenges, extending over decades. Consider services for children without families, whose predicament yields a risk extending well beyond a single adaptational episode. For these longer services, the proper analytic frame shifts from adaptation as a life episode, to adaptation as a life-cycle trajectory. The adaptational state remains central, but shows itself as a series of forks in a longer road. Many of the service decisions are similar, but the differences warrant noting. For example, in recent years a new strategy for service to the schizophrenic has emerged. This strategy illustrates the use of the "multi-episode frame" for reckoning the design of a service relationship expected to travel through years.

Many, perhaps most, schizophrenics apparently carry an inherited error of metabolism which alters the rate at which they can process important neurochemicals (see further discussion in Chapter IV). One illustrative formulation would suggest that the chemical foundation of schizophrenia in susceptible individuals is such that materials like epinephrine, nor-epinephrine and dopamine, which are basic to conduction of neuronal activity across synaptic junctions, and which are present in elevated amounts during the adaptational interval, apparently cannot be inactivated and removed from their points of action with ordinary and requisite speed. An associated line of research seems to show that these standard neurotransmitters consequently tend to collect during the episodes of acute disturbance and constitute the efficient cause of the altered behavior which characteristically punctuates the course of schizophrenia. It is abnormal amounts of these quite normal substances which alter the dynamics of events at the synapse in a way which consequently disorganizes behavior[52-56].

Several key points about the nature of this chemical predicament provide the specifications of the help that can be offered to afflicted persons. The underlying chemical situation, and the consequent risk of behavioral disorganization, are life-long. So the service strategy must encompass a similar term. But it is still true that the schizophrenic vulnerability becomes expressed at the time of a challenge that calls upon the individual to conduct substantial adaptational work. It seems that a life crisis draws out the episodically high flows of neurochemicals which create the condition of "decoupling overload" in the nervous system. Consequently, the behavior of the schizophrenic in crisis shows all the ordinary behavior any individual displays in such a period (see Chapters I and IV), but extremely enlarged and extended. So the resulting service design, although life-long in strategy, is episodic in tactics. Arrangements for the schizophrenic must, therefore, be set up so as to maintain continuity over decades, and yet allow for precise services during occasional adaptational overloads. Further, the service problem presents a call for both chemical and social subtlety because, although phenothiazine and butyrophenone medications significantly improve the adaptational work done by schizophrenics during acute episodes[56-58], such work otherwise moves in all its usual ways (see Chapter III). And it can fade in the face of undue interference by the circumstances of service. Chemical specifications arise from the duration, location and expression of the chemical problem. Social specifications arise from the form of a lifetime project which will fail if it recruits into asylum. Throughout its many-year span, the service aims to activate and repair any endangered social affiliations, in order that the regulatory context for adaptational work will be available during the inevitable challenges. Over a span of years, the design seeks to assure a precise intake of phenothiazine medications, at least during episodes, and in a manner which does not eclipse the priority of the pending adaptational activity. Finally, intrinsic to the overall style is the ability to readily switch from more intense to less intense styles of intervention as they become appropriate, and to effect such switching with minimal disruption of the fabric of a person's life.

Efforts to fulfill these requirements of design constitute a principle area of present experience. Consider two slightly different emerging patterns for the long-term care of schizophrenic persons—a family based, psychiatrist-centered pattern, and a lodge or group based, agency-centered pattern. When an individual resides with his family, the former pattern predominates. But schizophrenic persons show much less than average success in maintaining relationships with social groupings, including families, and consequently the family based pattern is possible with, perhaps, somewhat less than half of heavy-user schizophrenics. A steady decline in family linkage is seen during the adult years of the life of the schizophrenic. During their twenties, about two-thirds of known schizophrenics are living either with their parental family or the family they have established with a spouse. But by their forties, less than one-quarter are living within either type of family unit. Several factors seem to be at the base of this pattern of declining residence with kin. The schizophrenic is born into his first family, but it gradually becomes unavailable as his parents age and die. Equally important, schizophrenics are less likely to marry, and more likely to dissolve a marriage by separation or divorce[35]. Repeating or prolonged hospitalizations give rise to separations from relatives and yield a consequent additional toll on already fragile affiliational bonds. So in many situations, the pattern of long-term care of the schizophrenic begins with an early, family-based phase and later shifts to lodge-based arrangements. In some areas of the United States, lodge or clubhouse arrangements are underdeveloped and so the mid-life decline of the family system leads mainly into hospitalization or nursing home arrangements.

In both the family based, psychiatrist-centered pattern and group based, agency-centered pattern, similar observations in recent years make easier the task of deciding which are the more essential aspects of a successful design. In both patterns, many practitioners expect to manage the majority of episodes with short hospitalizations, or daycare[18] or homecare[58]. Further, management by such short hospitalizations, daycare or homecare results in better preservation of social affiliations, and in lower re-hospitalization rates than does service employing long hospitalizations[18,58/59]. In both patterns, phenothiazine medications shorten the acute episode[60] and reduce the frequency of acute episodes[61]. In both patterns, those individuals who remain in contact with a familiar social context between episodes experience fewer episodes[41,61]. The family based method of service is acquiring an increasing augmentation by social supports outside the family. Individuals who participate in outpatient, decision-oriented counseling, or in group based "drop-in centers," show more ability to maintain their family affiliations than do persons relying only on family resources.

Much of the current exploration in bettering the social supports for schizophrenics suggests that such group systems have aspects whose helpfulness has been tapped only slightly. For instance, groups of schizophrenics can construct a reliable pattern of meetings wherein they help each other with their current work of problem solving. Typical work at such meetings would include efforts to maintain employment, or efforts to assist a physician in the precise regulation of their medication. Many of these groups evolve sufficient stability to be termed a "club" or mutual-help group. The local chapters of Recovery Incorporated, for example, carry on exactly such problem-solving and affiliational activities[45].

Although most of such mutual assistance groups develop a pattern of regular meetings in a particular place, the groups differ in whether they encourage residing in the building where they meet. Because these group systems are relatively new, it is too early to make a confident judgment as to whether residence within the "lodge" or "clubhouse" is more or less helpful. At this time, most of the evidence favors the type of lodge-clubhouse developed by persons who live entirely away from the lodge in their individual residences. When the club members live in places apart from the clubhouse, the groups seem to endure longer and to exercise a more successful style for regulating problem-solving work. Many of the most successful lodges maintain an active schedule of daily activities, with governance and housekeeping by members, but ask their members to reside in a variety of other, nearby places.

The active-schedule, separated-domicile lodge seems to hold a remarkable potential for widening, rather than narrowing, the social excursion of its members. Perhaps for this reason, it may emerge as a useful way to provide a relatively long-lasting set of affiliations for its members, without propelling them toward asylum.

Guideline 17: The schizophrenic person needs enduring assistance in the maintenance of a set of affiliations provided in a manner which does not constrict his more general social excursion about the settlement.

MUTUAL-HELP GROUPS

RE-EMERGENCE OF CONFIDENCE IN MUTUAL-HELP GROUPS   In recent years, the activities of mutual-help groups have surged up with a distinctly renewed vitality. The term "mutual-help group" refers to those groups which form around a particular kind of problem shared by all the members—often a problem, such as alcoholism, drug addiction, etc., with which they cannot deal successfully apart from such a group. These groups ordinarily are separate from an individual's work, friends, family and daily associates. The individuals involved are drawn together and held with a cement that flows from the similarity of their predicament. For some, this bond is a function of timing—particularly the timing of their current distress. In most cases, a person will belong to a mutual-help group only for as long as distress exists, although some groups continue to assist each other with efforts almost as lasting as if there were bonds of kinship. Alcoholics Anonymous, Parents-Without-Partners and Widow-to-Widow are mutual-help groups. So are La Leche League and Synanon. Such mutually supportive groups are surely quite old as a component of civilization, but they now seem to be growing in importance as the family becomes smaller and as people move from settlement to settlement with greater frequency.

The security that man used to get from kin and clan—a security that enhanced his ability to adapt—he may now tend to seek in the company of those with whom he feels connected through a similarity of current experience.

The current re-emergence of interest in small-group activities as a dominant context for regulating adaptational work occurs partly as a reaction to a temporary movement away from such structures during man's recent experience with urban industrial life. Man may not have been fully aware of the importance of small-group activities in his life until his high migration rates and feelings of loneliness made clear to him the sense of social nakedness that can result. Individual migration almost inevitably carries the risk of such an interval of nakedness, at least during the time it takes to construct roots in the new place. And the role that the family and clan played in assisting with adaptational work may not have been visible until man experienced the frailty of solitary efforts. This frailty only showed itself after he stripped down to the nuclear family, moved to a small, highrise apartment or retired in old age to a setting where he had no social roots.

Another element that contributed to a temporary eclipse in the traditional reliance on such small groups is a factor that can be identified as "distress mislabeled as illness." Recent studies of normal human behavior during adaptational intervals (see Chapters I and III) have reminded us that distress is a necessary and intrinsic component of the signaling activities that organize the adaptational state and facilitate its social regulation. Earlier, several cultural factors had combined to yield a notion that such signaling might be apart from that which is usual and necessary, and might even be an illness. Perhaps man's natural longing to be free of distress became infused with a misplaced confidence that science, with its obvious successes in mastering some of man's problems, would be able to remove such anguish from his life. Such a view of life, which is unaware of the signaling value of distress, may also have played a role in drawing the medical profession into yeoman efforts to relieve distress with chemicals. That same life view may have drawn many to the belief, which is biologically peculiar, that ordinary adaptational distress might be a situation regaining therapeutic action. (See Chapter IV)

The never-quite-clear boundaries between events of distress and events of illness evoked even more perplexity when it became established that some categories of illness, particularly those associated with repeating depression, with schizophrenia or with hormonal disturbances like thyroid disease, do indeed lead to distress-signaling. Such distress-signaling, although altered, contains confusing similarities to that associated with ordinary adaptational challenges. For instance, it evokes social reactions of embrace and helping. And when man discovered that medical treatment and chemicals were distinctly helpful for some of these situations, that is, the situations involving altered physiology, it began to seem that more and more of the ordinary varieties of distress might be relabeled as illness needing treatment.

At present, we seem to be moving beyond this stylized definition of distress. A clearer realization is emerging that there are crucial differences between that distress which is associated with facing problems and that distress which arises out of altered body function. This realization has nourished a renewed interest in small groups as the ordinary line of assistance through which distress can be managed by conducting pending adaptational work. For example, worrisome levels of suspicion, sadness, perplexity or anger which might occur in an individual's life as he undergoes a loss, or as his situation changes in important ways, are being met with activities to find and use the proper kind of group. Ordinary distress is being more clearly viewed as a signal. On the other hand, seemingly the same distress, in which, however, the sadness or the perplexity remains *fixed*, or without relation to any external events that challenge equilibrium, is seen as more likely to arise out of abnormal body function or from social isolation. With such a fixity to his distress, the individual would be more likely to move into some category of professional service. It is being recognized again that ordinary signaling distress is an indicator that "Adaptational work is pending." Persisting displays of distress, or signaling outside a contextual challenge, are undergoing redefinition as a marker of "currently impaired adaptivity." Such reduced adaptivity would tend toward direct professional service or toward linkage with a regulatory group.

TYPES OF MUTUAL-HELP GROUPS   Mutual-help groups can be classified by the nature of the bond that draws their members together. The largest numbers of such groups are comprised of individuals who experience a similar problem or view of their problem. These are termed "predicament groups." When individuals are drawn together by a need for a temporary group which can regulate them until they are no longer actively in distress, or until they form an attachment with the proper kind of predicament group, they are using "bridging groups." A third type of group can form which is composed of individuals who are almost totally without connections to other groups. These persons have in common only the situation of social isolation and the experience of loneliness. They are sometimes brought together with the assistance of professionals during a brief interval when their affiliative interest is activated by a current crisis. Such gatherings are termed "professionally assisted mutual-help groups." They are truly mutual-help groups because, after a brief formative period, the professionals are no longer present. The group ordinarily evolves toward something that in every way resembles a set of persons united in common friendship.

Predicament Groups. The easiest type of group to form and the most persisting are predicament groups. The bond that can arise out of awareness of similarity of predicament can be strong. Many of these groups have the additional attractiveness of a reputation which broadcasts that the group has been useful to persons with an experience of a particular type. Predicament groups tend to concentrate on a central category of business which their members recognize to be closely linked with the problem they each share. For example, members of Alcoholics Anonymous identify patterns and attitudes which they suspect make it possible for alcohol to have destructive impact on their lives. First Friends is a group that helps manage the problems common to people who have spent significant amounts of time in mental hospitals. Parents-Without-Partners assist each other in managing the common problems in raising children and conducting family business that arise when, for whatever reason, there is no spouse.

A few predicament groups arise out of a category or distress which relates them incidentally to health professionals as well as to each other. These groups often see as part of their common interest a desire to relate constructively to the professional helpers in their lives. Such an interest is important to the activities, for example, of Recovery Incorporated, who are formerly hospitalized persons, and Synanon, who are persons addicted to a narcotic. Consumers-Action-Board, for example, is a group of current or recent heavy users of mental health services who are assisting each other in making the best use of such services. They see repeating problems within the challenge of returning to ordinary community life after long hospitalization. They add a component of political advocacy and bureaucratic expediting to their business.

Other predicament groups have little to do with any particular illness but share a common juncture with one of life's adaptational problems. La Leche League members share the problems of women trying to breastfeed their infants in a society where that practice is relatively infrequent. They assist each other in handling a situation where their mothers, friends and neighbors may be unfamiliar with the pertinent practices. The members of Greener Fields help each other face the problem of constructing a new definition of the purpose of their lives at middle adulthood, after the children are raised. Their lives may previously have been heavily occupied with domestic and familial business. Esklepieion is a group of prisoners and ex-prisoners who assist one another in formulating the problems of moving to life outside the prison. Beginning in prison, they help each other to practice a style of life that will be successful outside. Some members carry on continuing relations after prison until they are confident they have successfully managed the transition. Their relations may extend into a period of prolonged alumni status which arises out of affiliations based on the continuing similarity of their pasts and on their interest in helping others make an advance. Widow-to-Widow is a group of persons drawn together in the sharply defined context of the recent loss of a spouse. They assist each other in bereavement and in facing the problems of redefining self and circumstance. Members of Widow-to-Widow also show continuing affiliations after the management of the immediate crisis. Friendships formed in the heat of distress regularly broaden into recreational affiliations and into an interest in helping others in a similar circumstance. God's Clowns is a group of persons with cancer. Most are facing the problems of an illness which may very well take their lives, though they may now be in a remission. Although every person knows that his life will come to an end, members of a group like God's Clowns are particularly aware of mortality because they share the knowledge that the balance of their lives may be quite short. They assist one another in the tasks of drawing one's life into focus and of conducting certain categories of final business regarding children, family and property.

Bridging Groups. "Bridging groups" form a contrast to predicament groups. They provide a brief, regulative context for an individual in distress while a more enduring mutual-help group is located. Examples of bridging groups are the several kinds of "telephone hotlines" which exist in many settlements. These hotlines receive telephone calls from people in distress and assist in figuring the early stages of response. The characteristic feature of bridging groups is that they invite brief, immediate contact with individuals in distress under a wide range of circumstances. The invitation is extended particularly to those whose trouble is having a disorganizing impact on their lives. Many of these bridging groups are constructed around a telephone, "walk-in" or "drop-in" format. Their arrangements emphasize immediate availability and an uncategorical offer of, usually temporary, assistance. Bridging groups organized around a telephone line often display an advertisement including their telephone number in newspapers or other public media. The advertisement asks people who are contemplating suicide, or who are "coming apart," to call the hotline. Drop-in formats emphasize a room where people may come and discuss their distress without an appointment. The telephone services or drop-in services are often conducted by unpaid volunteers who take turns in handling calls and in talking with individuals presenting in distress.

Bridging groups ordinarily complete their contact with a person-in-distress within an interval of hours to days. They regulate an individual's chaotic distress for a sufficient period to assist him in resolving the situation, making contact with a professional agency, or entering a predicament group. Some bridging groups are organized around a particular problem or for a particular age group. There are, for example, suicide hotlines, rape hotlines, youth hotlines, older persons call-lines and drug-use hotlines.

Bridging groups have special usefulness to individuals who are in distress at a particular time when they are otherwise without any group that might assist them with pending adaptational work. Because individuals out of contact with family or friends are much more likely to experience a chaotic variant of distress, such individuals are similarly overrepresented among the users of hotlines. Social isolates, migrants and persons who have moved recently, including young adults who have left their family of origin but have not yet established their own conjugal family, are the principle users of bridging groups.

Individuals who present with a category of trouble not currently managed by the professional agencies of their particular settlement, are also overrepresented in hotlines. For example, problems associated with "overdosing" or recreational use of consciousness-altering drugs are dominant in many hotlines. So are problems associated with venereal disease. Because individuals who are not currently serviced by one of the agencies in the settlement are dominant among the users of bridging groups, such groups sometimes acquire a measure of counterculture and antiprofessional sentiment. For this reason, some bridging groups maintain only marginally cordial relationships with the professional agencies in the settlement. However, by and large, the trend is now moving in the other direction. Sometimes bridging groups ask public funds for the support, for example, of the telephone equipment for their work. Whereas even a decade ago they had trouble getting such funds, and in achieving necessary professional linkages, much of this turbulent phase of their growth now has past. Some of the telephone hotlines have attached themselves to one or another of the professional agencies in the settlement and may get support through that agency. Bridging groups and volunteer-served hotlines characteristically are regarded as helpful components of the helping resources of many communities. They are increasingly accorded respect and resources in line with the measure of their usefulness.

In many communities, telephone hotlines and bridging groups have an altogether remarkable amount of contact with individuals who are using chemicals for recreational or consciousness-altering purposes. The striking volume of this type of contact may arise because the use of such drugs may tend to disqualify individuals for the services of some agencies. But it is also possible that the use of such drugs may radically interfere with the conduct of ordinary adaptational work. It is quite a common experience in bridging groups and telephone hotlines to be contacted by individuals who are using mood-altering drugs and who, at the same time, seem greatly set back by a rather ordinary challenge. Such individuals appear less than usually skillful in gaining the assistance of those around them. On the other hand, the use of such drugs often places individuals in violation of laws, a

situation which may place additional difficulties on their getting prompt, precise service. In any case, the most usual
practice of bridging groups, when dealing with individuals
who are using drugs to alter mood, is to enter them into the
affairs of the bridging group long enough to get them off of
the mood-altering material and into a nonintoxicated state.
Then they quickly attempt to resolve the distress by stimulating problem-solving activity and by placing the person in
contact with one or another agency or mutual-help group.

Because of the likelihood that there will continue to be
both socially naked individuals and individuals whose trouble does not match the categories of service ordinarily available in the settlement, bridging groups would seem to face a
flourishing future. Bridging groups nevertheless will likely
continue to live in a twilight world between affiliated and
isolated people, between establishment and antiestablish-
ment, between legal and illegal, and between persons
viewed as being in-need-of-help and viewed as being in-need-
of-punishment. Because of a considerable measure of success
in temporarily regulating the adaptational work of their
users, such groups will continue to find a place in the overall
fabric of community life.

Professionally Assisted Groups. In contrast to bridging
groups and predicament groups, is a set of groups that have
nothing in common except that each one is composed of
isolated persons brought together partly through the action of professionals. These "professionally assisted
groups" often come into being only through the fact that they
are receiving service at the same time by a particular
agency. For example, the members may cluster as a side effect of attending a mental health clinic or a well-baby clinic.
Typically, the individuals whose bonding arises out of simultaneous agency attendance are without other social contact.

The background to this unusual variety of affiliation lies
in the enhanced attachment activity which operates during
the adaptational state (see Chapter I). A high percentage of
persons passing through a professional service are at the

same time passing through an adaptational interval. Even if they are social isolates, they will show a distinct, though temporary, readiness to affiliate. They are for the brief duration of the crisis interval more able to repair their status of social isolation. Most of these groups continue to exist around the edges of social agencies, as for instance, around the counseling work of clergymen or school counselors, or around outpatient clinics or hospitals. The new affiliations which these groups make possible for such socially isolated persons greatly increase the helpfulness of whatever other service they are receiving at the agency they are attending. Because socially naked persons are the major users of such groups, the groups often contain many elderly people, or migrants, or individuals whose protracted disability states have alienated them from other social networks.

Some of these groups receive a measure of continuing professional contact, expressed, for example, via an agency's provision of space for a drop-in center, coffee house or lodge for the use of individuals attending an agency for other service. Growing out of the clustering activities of people who use the coffee house, a mutual-help group may develop. Persons begin to attach to a group. They soon use the group to regulate and assist them with their problem-solving. Most often, the members move on to family groups or predicament groups as a more continuing context for their affiliations.

ACTIVITIES OF MUTUAL-HELP GROUPS   It is likely that the activity of mutual-help groups is expanding in scale because the groups provide an effective context for regulating adaptational work. Across all the diversity of such groups—whether they are temporary or enduring, or whether they are of the predicament type or bridging type, or whether they are professionally assisted or not—their shared focus is to assist with pending adaptational work. Mutual-help groups show a striking concentration on activities associated with starting, stopping, pacing, focusing and informing problem-solving work. Another remarkable element, given their diversity, is that the groups try to conduct their work without entering the individual into any special role as a patient or even as abnormal person. They center on helping an individual figure out what his difficulty is, and then what to do about it. They stimulate and troubleshoot the problem-solving process. Whatever the nature of the distress the individual presents, it is regarded as ordinary under the circumstance. It is seen as in no way abnormal. It is labeled as a kind of sideplay of "undone problem-solving" or as an indicator of a "need for doing some problem-solving." Because of the absence of any presumption of defect, the individual undergoes no loss of dignity nor of status by virtue of entering the group.

The groups assume that ordinary signals of distress, as for example, sadness or perplexity, are a salutary reason for joining the group. Operating in this manner, such signals yield the distinctly useful consequence of assembling and beginning the helping process. Signals of distress elicit other invitatory behavior from the group. The full range of panic signaling, of anguish, crying and shrieking, are met with invitations to join and work on problems. Perhaps one aspect of the attractiveness of the groups may be that presentations of signals of distress lead to contact and regulation rather than to chaos and isolation. An adaptational state which might otherwise be unregulated, prolonged or cycling is drawn into its ordinary purpose (see Chapter III).

It can be illuminating to see the dramatic change in an individual as he makes contact with a mutual-help group. He enters in distress, but is calmed when the group convenes around him. He enters in panic, but as the group engages with him he starts to define particular problems he will work on. He enters in perplexity, but as the group makes visible its "method," he begins to see tasks. He may enter in suspicion, wondering about the meaning of what is happening. But as the group reacts to the possibilities he mentions, he gets a beginning sense of what may be more likely to happen. He may enter in sadness, narrowly constricted in his contacts with people. As the group engages with him, he begins to visualize more clearly what is gone and needs replacement.

He can start to rebuild and move on with life. (See Guidelines Numbers 1 and 2 in Chapter I.)

When mutual-help groups are examined at a higher magnification, additional regularities appear in their activities. These regularities remind us again of the similarities that are common to all problem solving, independent of the problem being faced. For example, when an individual enters a group, the range of his attention and thoughts have that narrowness that is characteristic of persons-in-distress. He expresses a particular type of pain or repeatedly discusses a particular topic. As the group engages, there is a prompt increase in the breadth of his attention, in the number of matters he considers pertinent. He takes up new concepts for examining his predicament. There is a freshness to his search. This process is an example of "restarting the scanning attention." Such restarting is a characteristic consequence as an isolated, unregulated person-in-distress comes into contact with a group. (See Chapter I.)

The experience of self-identity undergoes similar changes in the context of the group. Individuals enter mutual-help groups with that diffused, vague identity typical of an individual-in-distress. As they move into contact with members of the group, one can hear questioning like, "Who are you," "I see you," "We like you," "Show us more." The individual responds, "I am feeling who I am," "I see myself," "I can recollect myself." This clarification of the sense of self-identity sometimes occurs after only brief contact. It is a gratifying experience to the members of the group as well as to the entering person.

The entering person often shows the loosened attachments to family, friends, projects and purposes that is characteristic of an individual beset with a major challenge. But as he enters the group he experiences at least one attachment—an attachment to the group or to individuals in the group. This new mooring brings an obvious calming. There is relief simply out of this contact. There is a new feeling of solidarity and dignity.

Mutual-help groups have distinct effects on a person's

behavior in ordinary social roles. An individual enters in distress showing deteriorated performance in the roles which define him socially, as breadwinner, friend, student. The group members note this deterioration, but typically envision it as temporary. They reflect on it primarily as a deviation from his more usual self. They do not see it as a statement of his essential, persisting self. By highlighting comparisons between this current state and a more usual, more desirable state, they arrive at "objectives for change." They define "steps in a plan." The changes in an individual's performance, as he is reminded of his usual more desirable self, can be quite dramatic. This role-enhancing, antiasylum posture of mutual-help groups constitutes a striking regularity, no matter how diverse they are in other ways.

The random-access memory, the "whir and blur," and the general experiences of internal disorganization that are characteristic of persons-in-distress, also change as the individual comes in contact with a group. The basic orderliness of method which is typical of these groups tends to stabilize the chaos of unregulated crisis. The great majority of mutual-help groups, especially those organized around a common predicament, emphasize use of "a method." For instance, Alcoholics Anonymous has a book. It has a set of practices for conducting meetings, a particular language and cluster of integrating concepts. The same is true of La Leche League and Recovery Incorporated. The group's method is often presented to members collectively, with a certain uniformity, and surrounded with sentiments of certitude and conviction. In consequence, the reacting individual begins to search his experience with a scheme rather than just being passively bombarded by it. He begins to develop a plan rather than just witnessing the impact of his predicament. Through the use of "the method" the groups very quickly turn a person's attention toward relieving distress by resolving some situation. Whatever the details of the method, it usually instructs the individual to search the problem, to appraise his options, to decide among them, to take action and to test his result. The resulting activities center on resolving the problem by decision and action in the real world, often by the development of skills the individual may not have used previously. The method tends to place an action-oriented perspective on the problem by offering a theory of how the problem happened, how to get rid of it and how life will be in the future. It tends to superimpose an orderly sequence of time onto the timelessness otherwise typical of the experience of distress. Since the method usually involves several contacts with the group, contacts extending well into the future, an individual is offered a reliable set of foreseeable events. For example, the method often regulates an individual's contact with the group by defining a set of important tasks and a necessary sequence. The method may explain to an individual, for example, that first he contacts the group, then is received and embraced. Then the group defines "help." Then the group offers help. Then the group explains those activities which form the method. Then they will offer their assistance in regulating the individual's movement through these tasks. Then the group offers to troubleshoot any difficulties that develop. Then the group helps the individual detect that the work has been satisfactorily finished. Then the individual may move into a helper or alumni status, or he may leave. The provision of such a sequence has the vital effect of starting, focusing, pacing and stopping adaptational work.

The large majority of mutual-help groups conduct many of their activities in the form of regular, patterned meetings. Most of the groups meet no less often than twice-monthly and no more often than twice-weekly in a particular place. They employ a set of standard mechanics for drawing their members together, making ready the place and conducting group business. They employ rules for the procedure of the meeting and for making group decisions. The groups ordinarily have access to a room with property and equipment. So, they have a need for continuing leadership and for a core group of individuals who provide continuity in an organization largely made up of temporary members. Even this basic group business has its effect on distress. Business conducted in an orderly way suggests to a distressed person that he is in the midst of a force of consequence and continuity. These effects are often visible within the first moments of contact and before any particular business has occurred.

Most of the groups employ one or another theory for explaining their method and concepts. Use of repeating conventions and special language often reaches levels approaching ritual. Typically the membership attaches to the method substantial amounts of belief and certitude. Professionals are sometimes chagrined by the quasi-religious component to this relation of the members to their method. What professionals sometimes overlook is that the risks of cult need to be seen in context with the risks of isolation. Further, many of the individuals in these mutual-help groups move beyond the ritual, beyond the method and beyond the group when it is no longer useful. But however the method would look when viewed through the conventions of science, it clearly has the effect of ordering the individual's chaotic experience when in distress, and of starting and focusing his efforts. Also, the method provides a way for individuals who have passed through the group before to add their experience to the group and to establish a persisting body of lore in reference to the problems the group faces.

The mechanics for conducting a meeting can be quite elaborate in mutual-help groups. This is especially striking if one considers the relatively temporary nature of many of the memberships. The mechanics for conducting meetings are often so developed that the observer is quickly impressed with the fact that orderly mechanics for the meeting have a significance beyond the actual conduct of the meeting. There is a standard way of opening the meeting, often with a speaking of words at the appointed hour. The leader is placed at the front and defines the agenda. The members report their recent experience before the group in the manner of a giving of testimony. For example, in the case of TOPS (Take Off Pounds Safely), the members "weigh-in" and report their headway in losing weight. In other groups, there is often an opening song and a reading from a book which contains "the method." Then the members are individually accorded recognition during the meeting for any headway they can report. Individuals who are not making headway are also identified. Immediately after the meeting, smaller clusters of persons form around these members to assist them in figuring why they are not making headway. There is often a speaker. The speaker's topic may have some relationship to the special interests of the group, but just as often it may be simply uplifting or diverting. The meeting often closes with a standard speaking of words. Then there is a social period, one with active, individual troubleshooting, often lasting longer than "the meeting" itself.

Mutual-help groups tend to show an earnest, optimistic focus on problem-oriented work combined with a focus on "bad news." When an individual is bringing in reports about his trouble, the members don't ignore such reports. They don't tell him that he is defective. They don't banish him. They regard reports of bad news as a central business of the group. This characteristic attention to "trouble-as-business" causes the group to attach to the problem-solving process, to try alternative strategies. It covenants the group to remain with the individual until his problem is delivered through whatever diversions may occur.

GENERAL EVALUATION   Mutual-help groups, whether of the predicament, bridging or professionally assisted type, are a topic of increasing professional interest. The product of their efforts looks good to professionals. Clearly it is attractive to the people who make use of such groups. Professionals are lately less apt to "look down their noses" at the groups. Members of the groups are less apt to look down their noses at the professionals. In an interval of only several decades, the relationship between professionals and self-help groups has evolved dramatically. Starting with a long phase of ignoring one another, they moved to knowing of one another, but disapproving. Then came a period marked by attempts by professionals to dominate the groups. At present, many mutual-help groups and many professionals appear to be moving into a phase of respectful commerce.

Basically, the groups may be considered a temporary

kind of social regulation for individuals who are temporarily bereft of regulation by virtue of the magnitude of their distress-signaling, by virtue of social isolation or by virtue of a condition of life with minimal affiliations. Mutual-help groups can provide a regulatory context for that interval in the middle part of adaptation, which is *after* the old way but *before* the new way. The groups appear to be societally instructive and worthy of expansion because they emphasize adaptive change rather than movement toward asylum. Because they are more part of the natural and continuing system of a community, and less a set of activities invoked from outside, the groups can sidestep many problems of power and authority. They are more like antibodies than like antibiotics. The increment in man's power to adapt which accrues when he is in the context of a regulatory group is of sufficient magnitude that he will find and use such a group when he can.

THE DECISION TO USE A GROUP   An individual-in-distress may be faced with the question of whether he should make contact with a particular mutual-help group. Professionals may have to deal with assisting an individual to move into contact with a mutual-help group. One cannot but be impressed with the relative precision of the pathways which quickly develop when professionals and mutual-help groups move into relations of open commerce.

The fact that an individual may or may not be suffering extreme distress is seldom an accurate indicator of whether or not a mutual-help group can assist him. Several other facts are more pertinent. If an individual does not have a memory defect, if he is aware of time, place and person in the midst of his distress and if he does not have false beliefs which he cannot detect are false, chances are that a trial with a mutual-help group is proper. Conversely, if an individual has a memory defect, or beliefs he cannot tell are false, or major weight loss, or no sleep for more than five days, or whenever there is a persisting practice of ablating distress by chemicals—under those circumstances mutual-help groups are usually not successful. In any case, if there is open commerce, the groups will send on to professionals those who do not constructively use the group. Mutual-help groups depend for their function on the fact that the individual's basic physiology is normal but his adaptational state needs regulation. Whenever there is doubt about the normal operations of the individual's physiology, the addition of the regulation of the group is less likely to work.

The plumage of distress is so often present in a situation where an individual is under challenge that its presence alone cannot be used to judge whether or not a mutual-help group will work. Changes in the distress plumage are highly important. If you observe the effect on the distress of another when you move into his life, when you help him figure out what is going on, you can make some inferences. You can assess the probable impact of social regulation. What is your own effect on the troubled person's problem-solving work? Does his signaling change? Does his signaling moderate? Does the topic-of-choice soften? Does the scanning activity of attention start? If so, the individual likely will benefit from a mutual-help group. Similarly, many people-in-distress show a less than usual attention to their eating, sleeping and grooming and to the maintenance of their affiliations. Those who regain a focus on the ordinary mechanics of survival when you move into relationship with them, are likely to be able to use a group.

WATCHING YOURSELF HELP ANOTHER   Because the regulatory activities of a helper, together with their effects on a person-in-distress, are at their base so automatic, the effort to become aware of them is accomplished only with directive effort. For similar reason, the fact of becoming aware of such activities offers little prospect of altering their performance. The measure of the advance is similar to that in becoming aware of one's breathing. Becoming aware of one's respiration does little to increase one's ability to breathe or alter one's success as a breather, at least in the short run. Even to become self-conscious about breathing may briefly interfere with the normal regulatory processes. There is something of the same quality to watching yourself helping. There is less a need to be reflective about what one is doing, than a need to feel your feelings and display your judgment. In spite of these disclaimers, there appears to be little harm in offering the following precepts:

1. *Be available for close contact and for being near a person.* Make eye contact. Make skin contact. Hear a person. Speak to a person. Speak slowly. Speak quietly. Face the person. Ask him to face you.

2. *Feel for a comfortable pace at which the person can enter and move through the situation.* Help the individual get rest, food, water and relaxation during his distress. Remember that the problem-solving effort may extend over days or weeks. It cannot all be done "now," though everyone may wish it so. Avoid chemicals as a way of helping a person get rest. Rather, use exercise, music, bathing and quietude to regulate a person's sleeping-waking and working-resting cycles. Move an individual "in and out" of his efforts. Do not hold him constantly onto his effort. Arrange for a "long-pull" endurance.

3. *Remark clearly on your reactions.* Know your thoughts. Report your observations. Trust in the value of your own vision of the appearance of things as a regulatory marker for the individual's efforts in consideration of his problem. Especially if the individual reports unreasonable ideas, speculates on careless action or seems to overlook main facts, reflect to him your reactions. React to unreasonable, careless or missing thoughts. Compare possibilities that the individual raises with your own thoughts regarding feasibility or precision. Reflect on the apparent attractiveness of the several future situations consequent to the several possible lines of action. Think aloud. Ask the person to think aloud. "Bounce" your thoughts back and forth without feeling required immediately to decide what is true, what is best.

4. *Reflect on descriptions of the past, the present, the future.* Place the current experience onto a line with what has happened before and with what may happen ahead. Help an individual remember what he was like, what life was like "before." Seeing what was "before" often helps visualize what may happen "after."

5. *Watch for isolation.* Hook the individual to other people. Watch for exhaustion. Hook the individual to a pace. Watch for stopping, cycling and repetition of thought. Hook the individual to a pathway.

These precepts are widely reflected in literature and common sense. They are much a part of the folk precepts offered to people-in-distress and to children growing up. One would not ordinarily regard them as explicit instructions for regulating adaptational behavior except in the context of an exploratory technical discussion of such behavior.

WATCHING YOURSELF HELP YOURSELF   What is next said here is not likely to be of much help to a person-in-distress. People who are in distress cannot at the time read books about how to help people-in-distress. Nevertheless, it wouldn't seem to interfere with the process to think, in advance, about helping yourself in distress. The same disclaimers that applied to watching yourself help another apply to watching yourself attempting to alter your adaptational behavior.

1. *What is the necessary pace of my efforts?* Regulate your expenditure of energy. Realize that it is unlikely that you will be able to handle the challenging circumstance in one day. You need to enter a rhythm of work and rest lasting over a several-week interval. Organize yourself to achieve the best product you can rather than the quickest product. Think of yourself as engaging with the problem, then conceiving possible responses, then collecting the best, then doing, then watching for outcome, then stopping, then resting. Imagine such a cycle as proceeding slowly, repeatedly, with the gradual accomplishment of the product. Realize that

all people-in-distress feel an urgency to their circumstance which is part of the process of activating the adaptational state. But also realize that regular efforts and repeating efforts are more likely to be successful than sudden, "all-out" efforts. Realize that exhaustion is the all-too-frequent price for an unregulated, quick run for the finish. To gain sleep when preoccupied with distress and anguish, take pains to divert yourself, to exercise. Ask others to distract you from your problem and to assist you in getting rest.

2. *Who are my helpers?* Make sure you have a person, or several people, to talk with at regular intervals as you move through the process. Keep in mind that although you may feel that you can face the difficulty alone, that there is a period in the middle of the adaptational interval when you will feel disorganized. You will not be what you were before and neither what you are going to become. There are risks of being stuck at this phase, or of not entering it because of the terror of it. Unwillingness to enter this middle phase forces you to remain unchanged. Ask yourself, who are my helpers? Name them. Keep your contacts open. Make sure you are going to be in contact with them regularly over the next several weeks. You do need not be in constant contact so long as you can be in repeating contact. They need to know, and you need to know, of that prospect.

3. *What is the future I desire?* Put yourself in touch with your values. As you move into an adaptational interval, you are going to have to figure out what is important, what baggage can be shed, what will need to be saved. You will need to define the attractive future you will organize to reconstruct. For that purpose, reflect on what are your sources of joy, and what the things are that you will like about yourself. In moments of quietude, reflect on what is important. Write it down. Convert it to statements describing how the future will be different from the current situation.

SUMMARY

In the nineteenth century, the socially regulative context, the connections between services and the enduring affiliations for individuals with long-term disturbances all were provided within asylum. In the twentieth century, practitioners are working to invent analogous arrangements without resort to asylum. How the system will eventually look is less clear than what it will have to do. It will have to enhance the adaptational work of those it would serve. It will strive to reinforce rather than eclipse the ordinary regulative fabric of human society. Doubtless, as the sciences of human biology and behavior advance, the technical activities of professionals will acquire more precision. And into this evolution, as far as we can peer, "the biosocial mechanics of adaptation" illuminate the story. And I hope my colleagues will be attracted to this recognition, so that out of our common understanding we might realize a greater measure of our desire to relieve those whose cry calls our presence.

VII

ACTION REPORTS

Many of the ideas discussed in this book have enjoyed a long history in human affairs. Notions concerning adaptation and its social regulation grow from long and penetrating roots, expressed even in folklore. Several such notions are central to the strategy of civilization. Much of the new excitement surrounding these old ideas comes from the fact that their recently expanded application in human services has resulted in distinct advances in the effectiveness of such services; and it is also exciting that this has been predicated upon a more open set of contacts between the natural sciences and psychiatry.

Several such notions occupy a central place in this book—as, for instance, "regularities in behavior during the adaptational interval," "the essential attachments" and "the social regulation of adaptational work." The four reports gathered in this chapter relate to the emergence of these particular notions as organizing principles in the work of a particular service organization, the H. Douglas Singer Zone Center in Rockford, Illinois. All four reports emanate from the activities of the staff of this facility. The reports were chosen because they reflect in a clear way the gradual recognition by this staff of the dominance of several "active principles" in their services.

REPORT ONE

THE WINNEBAGO AND BOONE COUNTIES SERVICE UNIT: A STEP IN LINKING THE SERVICES FOR A SETTLEMENT (MARCH 1967)

This report highlights the beginning of a local reception service and of an inpatient psychiatric unit. Both are directed toward enlarging the connections between other local services. In less than one year, the total usage of psychiatric hospital beds by the residents of the area markedly diminished.

SETTING AND PROBLEM   The H. Douglas Singer Zone Center, a facility of the Illinois Department of Mental Health, provides a portion of a local array of mental health services by assisting with inter-service linkages. The Winnebago-Boone Counties Service Unit of the H. Douglas Singer Zone Center is an inpatient and outpatient service relating to two counties in northern Illinois. It is not far from the population center of the area it serves. Winnebago and Boone counties comprise a combined population of 245,000 persons and are responsible for an average resident population of 515 persons in the Department of Mental Health hospitals, and an average 370 persons admitted yearly.

The typical patient who enters the Winnebago-Boone Unit shows distinct clinical mental illness, and is likely to be poor and lacking a job or employment skills. Often he relates to no family, or to one that is coming apart. In addition, he may be old, in trouble with the law, or lack skills necessary for living a satisfying life within any conventional social roles.

The system* of which the psychiatric patient is a part[1-9] includes himself, often the physiology of some inherited dis-

* The term "system" as used in this report refers to (a) a method for analyzing a problem: cataloging its parts, the setting and their interrelationships; (b) a method for designing a response to that problem, taking into account the relationship of the several parts to the whole; and (c) a method for monitoring, controlling and changing the response so it may continuously meet changes in the reality of the problem. System concepts provide a way for describing reality so as to conceive a certain "whole"

turbance, the physiology of adaptation, his problem-solving skills, his family, the groups of which he is a member and the particular health and social service professionals to which he might relate. It also includes his opportunities for social contact, education, employment, residence, purchasing power and income and a local environment of attitudes about casualty status. The system also includes judges, courts and police. The behavior accompanying his circumstances often brings him to the attention of these social agents. Their role in linking him to a system which can advance his adaptational efforts, or, alternatively, to one which can extrude him into a containment system, is crucial. The Winnebago-Boone Unit centers its activities on convening people and agencies that might relate to the patient's predicament and so, behave more as an adaptivity enhancing system.

METHODS   The Winnebago-Boone Unit has a staff of 39 persons with a psychiatrist as clinical director, and a social worker as administrator. It provides inpatient services in 30 beds, brief outpatient services (preceding, following, or in place of inpatient service), and activities to link the efforts of a network of agencies.

The inpatient phase of treatment consists of a socially activating environment with an average length of stay for all patients of 26 days. The staff work emphasizes an active testing of social skills, use of groups to assist with adaptational work, and phenothiazine and antidepressant medications.

Each person who is proposed to the staff by any portion

---

divided into "parts" in specified "relationships." The description aims to account for the behavior of the parts by resort to a very small number of relationships among the parts, or "states," of the whole. A system has a "boundary," includes certain elements which are "in" it, and excludes a much larger number of elements defined as "outside." The definition of system in this general way is similar to the following statement in other language: "The problem we are facing is composed of the following aspects . . . and any management of this problem will need to understand the following relationships between aspects of this problem...placed within the following environment...."

of this system (the patient, his family, a judge, a physician or another social agency) as being in need of inpatient care, is scheduled promptly for a reception conference. These conferences are held twice each morning and twice each afternoon. Their purpose is twofold: on the one hand, they identify persons who are in serious risk of institutionalization; on the other hand, they identify the network of persons and agencies that might be usefully linked into the predicament of this person.

An example of the role of such reception conferences can be given by the change in the system activity of the courts and judges. Until the advent of the Winnebago-Boone Unit, the mental health objectives of the courts were: (a) to receive distress messages from families and individuals, and reports of persons with grossly disturbed behavior; (b) to arrange for the apprehension, transportation and holding of such people; (c) to arrange for the examination of such persons by two physicians; and (d) when a sufficient number of persons had been certified as being in need of inpatient care, to transport a group to the nearest state hospital which was, depending on the case, 35 or 100 miles distant. The activities of the Winnebago-Boone Unit have encouraged an important modification in the system activity of the judges and courts. Judges continue to receive distress messages from family members and from patients, but instead of converting them into requests for commitment, they convert them into arrangements for reception conferences. The judge, along with the unit staff, insists that the patient, members of the family and representatives of involved agencies participate in such conferences. The family physician is often involved. If he cannot be present, he is included by conference telephone call so that he can be a party to the planning and assist with after-care arrangements.

The practice of convening the several parties in planning for a patient's predicament, including the judge, the family and the physician, yields a series of possibilities not otherwise available. Convening practices also allow for changes in the behavior of parts of the referral system. In general, the parts of the system develop a more intimate knowledge of each other's behavior and of the system aspects of such behavior. The courts now collaborate actively in convening the parties in planning for adaptive work to manage a problem. They show less interest in seeking a place to deposit troubled persons.

The judges learned of the operation of the conferences partly through discussions with Unit staff, and from patients and families. But a surprising step of growth occurred when the judges directly observed the conferences. They developed an appreciation for new issues in the complexity of the overall predicament, and an understanding of the Unit staff's strategy of appraising the problem and of assisting with adaptational work.

THE EXPEDITER   The mental health expediter is a staff element in the design of the Winnebago-Boone Unit. The expediter attends reception conferences and records those elements of the patient's predicament for which complicated, extra-institutional arrangements may need to be made. Such arrangements might include entering job training, assisting with getting a room in a boarding house, drawing the patient into an after-care group or helping him get a job. The expediter establishes target dates for completion of the several tasks, and starts on them immediately at the time of admission to service. He links a system to a troubled person.

A FOCUS ON "BRIDGING" GROUPS   During the inpatient and outpatient phases of service, many patients are linked to transitional, or "bridging," groups. Most of such groups are of relatively short duration. They may come together for eight to ten sessions over several weeks. They are task-centered on identifying problems, using group discussion and asking the group reaction regarding decisions that may be pending.

Some patients, particularly heavy users of service, are not now members of groups. Such persons experience notable difficulty in using groups. The Unit, therefore, established "spin-off groups," an approach to assisting the affil-

iational efforts of socially isolated persons. Spin-off groups
have ten to twelve members, meet eight to ten times, and
quickly learn such functions as "convener," "arbiter," "social
chairman," "recorder," etc. These groups are helped to become a collectivity that can function without a staff member
present, so as to provide a setting where persons otherwise
without a group may help each other with adaptational
work. Many of these groups do not actually spin off to independent function. But, in the process of forming an *ad hoc*
group, the members learn to allocate the various jobs that
need to be done and to set up conventions for conducting
group business. Such activities by the members reactivate
their affiliational interests, even when they may have been
dormant for a long time.

MECHANICS OF RECEPTION   The officer of the day is a member of
the Unit staff charged for a period with receiving all requests
for service. It is his responsibility to determine whether
there is a serious possibility that the person in question risks
being institutionalized, and what services should be linked
to this individual. He also works to discover the first opportunity when the necessary persons can be convened. He
makes arrangements and convenes the conference. He is
charged with drawing from the conference the data necessary to the assessment of the situation. He arranges for such
special examinations as the psychiatrist may need.

DISCUSSIONS WITH CITIZENS   Efforts to establish a constructive
set of relationships with the residents and agencies of the
pertinent localities are a major activity of the Winnebago-
Boone Unit. The Unit regularly considers its service policies
and services designs in discussion with a local mental-health-
planning authority. It works to create a growing group of
persons knowledgeable about any poor connections between
services, and about other problems which may lie within the
casualty management system. With the several citizens'
groups, the staff examines: (a) the types of calls received by
the officers of the day; (b) the disposition of such calls; (c) the

repeating types of troubles reported by persons admitted to services; (d) problems in finding longterm arrangements for care and rehabilitative services for persons with complex packages of trouble; and (e) problematic agency policies, insurance provisions, etc.

APPARENT REDUCTIONS IN INPATIENT SERVICE   The risk-group being serviced by the Unit is the same one, as closely as we can know, to that previously cared for by the several state hospitals of the area. Any person from Winnebago or Boone counties who now requires inpatient care, and is admitted to Department of Mental Health inpatient care, has begun to be admitted exclusively to the Winnebago-Boone Unit. The state hospitals no longer may admit directly. Patients arriving directly at state hospitals are promptly transferred to the Winnebago-Boone Unit[10]. The average age of persons previously admitted to the Elgin and East Moline State Hospitals from Winnebago and Boone counties was 42.2 years; the average age of persons now admitted to the Winnebago-Boone Unit is 41.5 years. The average length of stay of persons who were admitted to Elgin and East Moline State Hospitals was 38 weeks; the average length of stay for persons now admitted to the Winnebago-Boone Unit is 26 days. The package of trouble with which patients arrive appears to be the same: clinical symptoms, poverty, lack of job skills, deteriorated social skills, absence of a family or a small-group support network and absence of a place of residence.

Because of the cooperation of the courts, social agencies and families in the reception conferences, the treatment power of the 30 beds of the Winnebago-Boone Unit appears equivalent to the 420 or more beds of the Department of Mental Health formerly occupied with the care of the same population. The cost of operating the Winnebago-Boone Unit is about $60 a day, allocating a fair fraction of the administrative costs of the larger agency of which it is part. The daily costs at the state hospitals it replaces approximated $6 a day. However, the length of stay in the Winnebago-Boone Unit is less than one-tenth as long as the previous hospitalization. The cost per episode of residential service is therefore about the same. The social effectiveness seems much better with the Winnebago-Boone Unit. The patient is more likely to be kept as a member of the family, or to be kept on the job if he has one. The process of removal to distant places may be being aborted at an earlier point.

REPORT TWO

THE MENTAL HEALTH EXPEDITER: A FURTHER STEP IN LINKING THE SERVICES IN A SETTLEMENT (DECEMBER 1967)

The role of the psychiatrist in organizing steps toward biologic correction of a disorder is well known. Because mental disorder often yields a range of profound social disturbances, a variety of types of co-workers is emerging to assist the psychiatrist use and repair the social context. This report discusses the development of one such co-worker, the expediter, whose role combines activities similar to administration with ones similiar to counseling.

GENERAL CONCEPT   The mental health expediter fills the same function as the expediter in industry, except transferred to a mental health service setting. The idea in both contexts is much the same: the expediter coordinates a number of events to see that they happen, and in such a manner that an overall good outcome occurs.

Expediter functions are discussed by Reiff and Reissman[11]. The value of the expediter they ascribe to lessening problems caused by the fragmentation of health and welfare services in many communities, and to the social sequelae of illness[11]:

The expediter is a link between the client and community resources. He maintains a roster of service agencies within the community. He knows what type of service they provide and their rules and regulations. He main-

tains contact with these community facilities. He gets to
know the personnel who can facilitate referrals, and he
keeps a relationship with them. He is the instrument
through which interagency referrals are made. He exercises tracer and follow-through procedures to see that
the client makes appointments and is receiving the maximum potential service of an agency with minimum delay. He receives complaints from the client about service, and investigates them in the client's interests. He
provides the professional members of the service team
with information about what resources are available
which might meet the needs of the client as defined by
the professionals. He takes responsibility for facilitating whatever disposition the team makes. He inter-
prets his role to all agencies, services, and to the community generally.

GETTING STARTED IN NORTHERN ILLINOIS   In March 1965, the administration of the Singer Zone Center advertised for mental
health expediter candidates in the following language:

> In the Rockford Zone of the Illinois Department of Men-
> tal Health, and at the H. Douglas Singer Zone Center, the
> expediter is a person trained in any of the mental health
> disciplines who coordinates available service, whether
> inpatient, outpatient, or home care, and whether in pri-
> vate or public agencies, so as to focus it on a goal. He has
> responsibility to implement those parts of the program
> for the troubled person which (a) will go on outside of
> the Singer Zone Center or (b) which involve the collabo-
> rative efforts of several people or several agencies. He is
> asked to develop effective arrangements for attaching
> people to families and for involving them in a plan to
> engage an individual at a maximum contribution to the
> community.

In the summer of 1965, the Rockford Zone Director and
the President of Northern Illinois University, which is within commuting distance of the Singer Zone Center, had joined
to co-sponsor a two-year training program for the mental

health expediter. The expediters would receive a Master's Degree in Guidance and Counseling at the University. A year of academic work would be followed by a year of practical field experience at the Center. The National Institute of Mental Health granted support for three years of training programs, and asked the University and the Center to work toward a more precise curriculum and to evaluate the effectiveness of the expediter in the service function.

In May 1965, an advertisement was placed in the *Peace Corps Volunteer's Career Information Bulletin.*

> The Illinois Department of Mental Health, in cooperation with Northern Illinois University, invites applicants from Peace Corps volunteers for a work-study program leading to a Master's Degree and to skills in serving the mentally ill, the mentally retarded and the social offender. The training program involves one year's academic work at the University and one year's precepted experience at the H. Douglas Singer Zone Center. Study areas emphasize management of crises in human lives with a more precise recourse to residential and institutional modes of care. The work-study program offers training in social service practices and opportunity to explore ways for families and communities to embrace persons with disabilities.

In September 1965, the first class of 23 expediter trainees started the academic year. It was planned that they would join the service operations of the Center in September 1966 for the precepted service year. The Winnebago-Boone Unit of the Center started its operations in October 1966, and had planned to have expediters exercise a central function in its mode of operations.

TRAINING DESIGN   In the early planning stages, the essential ingredients in the training program were thought to be as follows: (a) a Master's Degree for career-line potentiality; (b) a behavioral-science, inter-disciplinary, professional appraisal system; and (c) beginning task experience in the operations of the health, welfare and rehabilitation sector of the economy.

The academic year included didactic work in psychology, principles of counseling, the biology of the adaptational state and the sociology of the health and welfare sector. Classwork also emphasized descriptive psychopathology, group process, group disorganization, features of human growth and development and several theories of personality. The course-work also introduced the topic of evaluation of health service operations, using courses in statistics, techniques of research, a research seminar and a modicum of experience in independent research.

A practicum of field experience was arranged for one day per week at the Center and in selected other agencies in the territory. On the days of the field experience at the Center, case-centered discussions were held on the following topics: (a) a definition of mental health; (b) adaptation and its relation to health and illness; (c) service organizational problems: assessment and change techniques; (d) development of the personal identity; (e) cultural background to individual health and illness; (f) diagnostic nomenclature; (g) personal attachments and affectional systems; (h) grief and separation events as a model for health and illness; (i) the repeating offender against the law; and (j) patterns of disability management, with characteristic types of cases.

A major emphasis was placed on counseling technique and its use in life crises. It was felt that the expediters would need a professional identity for relating to their clients that would be different from therapist and different from friend. A particular method for conceptualizing crises was taught that emphasized the flexibility and possibility for growth during crises, and that attempted to loosen any stereotyped ideas that mentally ill persons are necessarily unable to deal effectively with their troubles[12]. The expediters were taught some background of the physiology and behavior of people during the adaptational interval, in order that they might have a professional appraisal system with which to assess the severity and phasing of a crisis response in a client. The expediters were offered several percepts for counseling in crises: (a) circumscribe the problem in time, space and life area; (b) avoid, if possible, removing the patient from responsibilities of life; (c) participate with the client in the cognitive organization of the problem; (d) limit the duration of the encounter, structure it rigidly; and (e) focus on decision, action and testing of the results of such action.

The expediters were taught Lindemann's description of the symptomatology and management of acute grief[13]. The expediters would be seeing a number of people in grief reactions, and could explore bereavement patterns as a focus for understanding healthy, and less healthy, ways of responding to life challenges[12].

Emphasis was also given to understanding the social breakdown syndrome as described by Gruenberg[14]. Many of the patients whom the expediter would be attempting to help might be in various stages of such a process. Understanding social breakdown as a process, with identifiable causes and regularities in its development, has seemed to make it possible for the expediters to engage intensely with their clients without getting overly angry, anxious or discouraged.

A major emphasis in training was placed on skills in "social linkage," and on methods for making, strengthening and altering such links. The expediters distinguish four grades of link: (a) an *information link:* information is given to the patient about agency services, addresses, job information, etc.; (b) *a monitored contact:* the expediter follows the patient to the extent of making sure that he arrives at a certain place, or makes contact, or takes the action which initiates a critical link; (c) *monitored effectiveness:* the patient is followed for a longer period of time; the link is altered or re-cemented as necessary; and the expediter acts as a troubleshooter to see that it remains established, strong and effective; (d) *community and family embrace:* the linking process is carried a further step toward attitudinal change on the part of family and portions of the community. A person formerly felt to be dangerous, offensive or unwanted is found useful, interesting and belonging. The expediters show a continuing interest in conceptualizing social linking. Linking technology is, in fact, their own kind of professional expertise.

CASES   The expediters conduct three main kinds of activities: (a) the officer-of-the-day (OD) responsibility, an attempt to organize the precise use of services for seriously ill persons; (b) operations to arrange continuity in the care of the person through the phases of reception, inpatient, outpatient and release; (c) operations focused during the interval of time when persons are re-entering the community after long stays in institutions.

Case 1. The expediter was involved in reception, assessment, continuity and troubleshooting in Case 1:

A 52-year-old father of five, with several hospitalizations for depression and the physical effects of heavy drinking, was admitted for 22 and 7 days each within the past 18 months. He was first seen in jail, where he showed sadness, suicidal ideas and poor physical condition. His history revealed ordinary skills and productivity, but abuse of alcohol had resulted in loss of employment and separation from family. An expediter in the OD role set up a reception conference with the patient, his wife and daughter. Admission to inpatient care was arranged as the first step in a plan. A job search was started. Links were established with an Alcoholics Anonymous (AA) "visiting sponsor." The expediter helped the patient arrange for temporary public assistance and temporary residence in a boarding house. After discharge from inpatient care the patient lost his first job. A second job in a nursing home, with residence in the same home, worked out well. Follow-up visits show that the patient is employed, not drinking, in AA and occasionally visits his family. The expediter receives continuing information by phone and postcard.

Case 2. Expediters are involved frequently in situations at the transition from long hospital care to more ordinary settings, as in Case 2. Present in this case are the elements of counseling, monitoring and continuity, focused on the problem of transfer from prolonged inpatient service.

A 57-year-old domestic worker and widow, with a diagnosis of schizophrenic reaction, had experienced three previous admissions of one, three, and six years each. This current discharge from the state hospital was coordinated by the expediter staff of the Winnebago-Boone Unit. The plan involved residence in a boarding home. After several months, the expediter noted that the patient had few friends. With counseling, the patient decided to move into a sheltered care home and took employment in the same home, a situation offering more social contacts. She has developed strong, helpful social roles there, and on periodic visits shows advancing job performance.

ROLE OF THE EXPEDITER   Expediters conduct their OD, reception and continuity functions through basic, practical tasks. They help a patient find a job. They assist in finding a suitable place to live. They facilitate the making of decisions, particularly decisions to move ahead in life; the expediters help a person review where he is, where he wants to go with his life and what the next steps can be. They help a person take action to make concrete changes in his everyday circumstances, in his family structure and in the important relationships in the family or social units of which he is a member. The expediters work to precipitate the *occasion* of decisions, facilitate the *clarity* of the decision, move the decision toward *action* and monitor the *results* of that action. The expediters check back on plans to see how they are going. They set up regular telephone reporting or postcard reporting by their patients so the latter can let them know that things are going well or badly.

THE EXPEDITERS THEMSELVES   The expediter group is young. The median age in the first group is slightly over 27 years, in the second group, 26 years, and the third, 32 years. The age range is from 23 to 62. There are 23 men and 20 women in the three groups. Slightly less than half come from backgrounds in the Peace Corps. For the most part, their previous backgrounds were in social service or teaching.

RELATIONS WITH OTHER WORKERS   When the expediter role was first discussed in Rockford in 1964, some local agency personnel spoke of the proposal in quite negative terms. They referred to the proposed expediters as "low grade social workers," "untrained psychotherapists," or "high grade volunteers." As the program evolved, the expediters generated considerable respect in other agencies. Now they are regarded as quite helpful people. The expediters do not have a professional organization but are invited to meetings of social workers, rehabilitation counselors, and interdisciplinary mental health lectures. They are formally invited to many community planning discussions. They have a view of the health and welfare sector in the territory which may be more complete than that of many other workers. This may be because the expediters move in a domain which involves them with almost every agency in the territory and in a variety of roles.

USE IN OTHER SETTINGS   The expediters have turned out to be such an inventive, effective group that they have been asked by other staff on the units on which they serve to do many things, from general administration to psychotherapy. Some of the expediters have moved from the expediting function into these other useful functions within the overall operations of the Center. The linking function and continuity function are emerging as the core elements of the role.

The persons who operate the expediter project believe that four criteria need to be met before the mental health expediter is useful in a particular setting[15]:

1. The expediters need specific training, plus a career line credential such as a Master's Degree, the latter to protect

them from the relatively atypical nature of the role at this time.

2. The staff of the institution within which the expediter works needs to understand the expediter function as a linking, counseling and continuity agent. The senior staff needs to understand how to support these functions administratively.

3. The other agencies in the local field of operations need to understand the function of the expediter. Such understanding can result from pertinent inter-agency planning.

4. The leadership of the agency from which the expediter works needs to appreciate the task of maintaining an activist, stereotype-loosening approach to the expediter's work. Otherwise there is a danger that persons in these innovative and unprotected roles might become burned out. Without nurturance, the functions of linking, continuity and counseling quickly deteriorate into the related mechanics of referral, record keeping or transportation.

REPORT THREE

DECISION COUNSELING: ADVANCING SERVICE THROUGH A BETTER USE OF THE ADAPTATIONAL INTERVAL (NOVEMBER 1969)

Whereas the first report focused on an administrative design, and the second on a role formulation, this third explores a clinical method. Decision counseling is an example of a clinical approach directed to the relief of those symptoms which frequently arise from aborted or prolonged adaptational behavior. The method is directed toward starting, pacing and focusing adaptational work. Relief, when it occurs under these circumstances, results from the ordinary termination of the adaptational state along with the resolution of whatever initiated the state.

CLINICAL ADVANTAGES Professional interests highlighted in crisis work are management of an individual in his ordinary social situation, or with minimal removal from that setting, together with prompt, brief services and a more precise concept of the use of institutionalization. Management in ordinary social position, when possible, helps maintain a person's integrity in his usual social system following the passage of the adaptational interval. Constructive use of key people from the social network sometimes aborts the social mechanics of extrusion. Arranging the treatment system so as to achieve close timing between precipitating events and the entry of help takes maximum advantage of the distinctive pattern-erasing physiology of the adaptational state. Minimal use of institutionalization and environmental controls enhances the likelihood of a skill increase during crisis, and of an adaptational solution pertinent to ordinary environments.

Decision counseling is central to several clinical methods addressed to the improvement of social skills during crisis. Decision counseling method has usefulness in crisis because it can be employed quickly in or near the setting where the person lives. It can usefully involve members of his social network. It can take advantage of the ordinary problem-solving processes which maintain health[16/17]. The method makes maximum use of the turmoil of crisis to establish new patterns of thought, and of the usual disruption of affectional attachments to establish more effective attachments. Decision counseling is directed to the cognitive and affectional changes possible in crisis and is pertinent to the classical professional objectives of altering personality structures toward more competent life patterns.

REGULARITIES IN ATTACHMENTS   It is a major premise of decision counseling method that ordinary life involves a stable arrangement of transactions between the self and the environment that are necessary to the self, not incidental. It is a corollary that the self atrophies when these attachnents are severed. Necessary attachments include: (a) food, construction materials and stimulating information; (b) a clear identity or self-view; (c) affectional attachments to a small number of persons; (d) persisting linkage with a group as member; (e) opportunities for dignity and self-esteem deriving from role performance; (f) notions of the good life and of a comprehensive system of meaning; and (g) attachment to the economic system of the community. Acquired patterns of perception and thought guide these transactions. Wallace calls these stable patterns for managing the environment "the mazeway," and discusses operations of the mazeway in steady states[18], in crises[19], in illness[20], in social innovation[21], and in disasters[22].

REGULARITIES IN CRISIS Spiegel[23], Tyhurst[24], Carlson[25], Visotsky[26], and Naftali[27] consider the special properties of cognitive and affectional attachments as they may be characteristic during an adaptational interval. Persons-in-crisis typically experience a narrowed span of attention, focused on the anguish of the state, and repetitively offer ruminative reports of a few features of the situation. Perceptions of a threatened loss of influence over the situation call up the anxiety-fight-flight-vigilance posture and signals of distress. A marked reduction in the usual amount of stability of perceptions shakes the experience of identity, or self-sameness-through-time, and promotes an impulsiveness to behavior which can abort the opportunity for the systematic operation of standard problem-solving cognition. In the emotional lability of crisis, people reach out for affectional attachments old and new, and can change or increase their effective social network. Diminished awareness of a life strategy notion, and resultant lack of clear orienting attitudes, foster a characteristic lack of perspective about the scale and nature of the current trouble. The typical diffusion of identity notions during crisis makes the expectations of the observer, or helping person, critical in forecasting what kind of persisting identity will be developed. Stereotyped expectations, injected by the observer, about the longterm, old, repeating, schizophrenic, alcoholic or retarded patient, exert a powerful effect in altering the outcome. Projections of the possibility of improved outcomes, and of higher levels of coping skills, seem equally powerful[21,25,26,28].

ORDINARY ADAPTATIONAL WORK   The properties of the thinking and feeling life during crisis which are so distressing are also the basis for the remarkable biologic adaptivity of the period. And they form the background for decision counseling. Techniques for problem solving, when identified are learned rapidly. The fund of information is prominently and surprisingly fully available, except in the most overwhelming crises, but in a disorganized way. Portions of information usually excluded from awareness suddenly pop into mind, and familiar notions are expressed less prominently. *When the usual calculus of reckoning is disturbed, a special process of search, appraisal, decision and action begins. The search for the boundaries of the problem proceeds to an appraisal of movable or masterable features. Decision among feasible options moves to a test of success in implementation.*

The search-decision-test sequence is a process of central survival importance to man, and not dependent on the particularity of "the problem." The different circumstances of death, illness, disaster, social change and separation from loved one contain a common property—bereavement of a cherished, now lost, life pattern. Bowlby[29,30], Wallace[19], and Lindemann[31] describe the generic loss response. The absence of the old object elicits search or "reminiscence" behavior. The construction of a new object shows characteristic "perplexity" behavior. Beginning use of the new object shows "testing" behavior. The similarity in the responses to such diverse types of losses suggests an underlying, elemental shift in the style of relating to the environment from "steady state" to "adaptational." A substantial fraction of the crisis plumage is but an extension of behavior that is common to any adaptational interval.

The cognitive events during adaptational work offer the basic focus used in decision counseling. In the creation of new objects of thought, a group of "facts," or pattern discriminations, become grouped into a unit. After assessing the relationships of a "situation" to the rest of the life space, the individual molds it into a decision model. He selects among options for managing, "or handling," the fact. The familiar appraisals, "danger is present [crisis-in-transit]," "facing the problem [search for management options]" and "it's okay," or "there is still trouble" [outcome monitoring], exemplify social signals used to let other people know what aspect of the adaptational process is active, or "how it is going." These elemental problem-solving skills and signals make up White's concept of "competence[32]," Skinner's concept of survival control behavior[33]," and comprise several of the clinical markers used in Ruesch's method for the assessment of social disability[34].

CLINICAL APPLICATIONS Counseling is central to many psychiatric clinical skills, and has received abundant didactic attention. Four points are worthy of emphasis:

1. *The setting is pertinent to the outcome:* Glass has highlighted the World War II and Korean experience in the management of combat performance crises[35/36]. The use of counseling and a high degree of performance expectancy, in or near the individual's peer network, has enormous productivity in comparison to other methods. The exploration of new behavior which masters real life difficulty is the objective. Therefore, a current life setting that allows testing of new skills is important. The setting in which the crisis is resolved is likely to be the one later found comfortable to the individual. Institutional settings and ordinary settings each promote different "solutions" and "locations of choice" after the resolution.

2. *The perplexity and doubt characteristic of crisis can often be converted to a decision to try for the gratifications surrounding problem-managing behaviors.* The homeostatic forces of personality ordinarily promote a tendency to return to old ways after the perturbations brought on by life. New information is ordinarily reconstructed to make each part of the continuing drama look somehow like the previous scene.

The homeostatic personality process is an important force. The decision counselor attempts to couple it to the search-decision-action sequence by noting and naming any beginning adaptational work which occurs, and by linking it with the individual's identity and self-picture. The counselor places his own focus of attention on behavior linked with the adaptational sequence. He is inattentive to other behavior. The method of selective attention is especially effective during the expression of the pattern-erasing physiology of the crisis interval. The identity deployed by the person in crisis is, to a substantial degree, that portion of the identity noted and reflected by the counselor.

During intervals of chaos and overwhelming trouble, an individual frequently makes a fixed, pessimistic outcome prediction. The counselor can act to keep the situation flexible by maintaining a respectful expectancy that competent responses may be found. Often he can embolden adaptational operations simply by marking those aspects of a person's life and world view that the individual deems important. The counselor can undercut the homeostatic power of fixed-outcome beliefs by acknowledging that, although they may be true, some people doubt them and other beliefs are possible. Simply casting surprise, or doubt, onto predictions made by the troubled person, or by persons around him, can "uncouple" attitudes expecting incompetent behavior.

3. *Convening key people belonging to the troubled person's social network into the background of the counseling relationship can sometimes greatly increase its innovative power.* Bringing together persons who have affectional attachments or key daily roles in relation to the troubled person makes the operating social field more visible and more unitary. Persons in turbulent, stressful degrees of trouble may be using impulsive or visibly incompetent patterns of behavior that have had an alienating effect on his network. Persons convened in crisis may experience a distinct renewal of attachment feelings. Also, the people in a troubled person's network may develop a dramatic new awareness of

their conjoint impact on a person's predicament. Constructive changes often evolve from this category of new information, one that can often only be developed at a convening. Dignity, status and self-esteem are enhanced. The individual is provided an opportunity for his dignity to become coupled with a competent handling of the difficulty.

The counselor provides social contact by moving intermittently into the presence of the person in difficulty. The fact of this presence can promote a more extensive inventory of options, perhaps by keeping the person-in-trouble connected to a social system. The counselor signals that his membership in this process is brief, and the decision process itself, as handled by the participants, is the central event in any adaptational change.

4. *The usual counseling activities—defining the problem, specifying the possible courses and figuring the proper method of decision—are sufficiently reliable for the counselor to report their likely helpfulness to the troubled person.* Frequently, interest is enhanced by such a report. The desired outcome is problem-solving behavior designed by the troubled person, which is pertinent to the predicament at hand. To this end, the counselor focuses attention on (a) an energetic inventory of the elements of the predicament; (b) an innovative specification of the options; (c) a precise decision model for selecting from among the options; (d) occasions to test the decisions; and (e) assessing the outcome, and starting over when necessary.

Counselors often find that the mood and emotional life undergo dramatic improvement as decisions are made, especially decisions which have been pending a long time, or about which the individual has been frightened or pessimistic. Changes in major features of a life situation precipitate a "new look" to things, and an activism which is directly gratifying to the patient. Because the decision counselor's view of the options may be larger than the view of the person in trouble, new options can be viewed and can introduce a gratifying flexibility to the situation. Introducing more options for consideration enlarges the opportunity for change already present in any adaptational interval.

CASES   *Case 1* illustrates decision counseling involving a mentally retarded young man, his family and a court. It took place in connection with a reception conference.

This 24-year-old moderately retarded young man lived with three other siblings in the family of a skilled machinist. He was arrested on a complaint of molesting a five-year-old girl. The girl's parents were former neighbors. A decision-counseling session was held in his home the day after the arrest. It included the counselor, the patient and the parents. The counselor arranged the session in the home so that all participants would recognize that there was a range of options other than institutionalization clearly in view. He convened the whole family to foreshadow the fact that some options might involve a unitary family response. Under the counselor's focus of attention, the group made a historical review of the patient's life, previous difficulties and current predicament. Inquiry was focused around identification of steps that the patient could now take. In four sessions, a program was selected by the patient involving (a) daily attendance at a sheltered workshop; (b) a private reading tutor; (c) biweekly public school classes in reading, writing and arithmetic; (d) more weekend family group activities; and (e) his presenting his plan at a competency hearing 60 days hence. During the hearing, the family expressed the belief that a more organized life might improve the situation. The patient was declared legally incompetent to stand trial, but taking hold of his predicament sufficiently to make considertion of incarceration unnecessary.

This case illustrates that decision counseling can relink a person to his social network during the flexibility of crisis. The site and timing of the conference likely are critical to the outcome.

Case 2 illustrates decision counseling started during inpatient care, continuing through outcare and home care. It highlights the usefulness of helping an individual to manage major distress, as for instance, on the occasion of the loss of a beloved person.

An unmarried, 45-year-old plant administrator requested admission to the alcoholism unit after detoxification in a local hospital. The patient started decision work on the third day with a life review which suggested a pattern of few friendships. He had loved a woman who would not move with him when he changed location ten years ago. After this loss he constricted social activity to two friends at work. Nine months before admission, one of the two was killed in an auto accident, following which the patient's use of alcohol increased markedly. His performance on the job declined. The review of current problems focused around the desirability of joining in some new groups and activities and exploring other options for current action which might be responsive to the patient's judgment that he had met each of a series of losses by further restriction of already scarce social opportunities. Anticipating that the patient would also mourn the eventual loss of his relationships with treatment staff, the patient and counselor proceeded with mourning counseling. Systematically, they noted the experience of the comfort of being with someone during the distressing work of problem-solving and other helpful aspects of the current counseling relationship. Next, they named replacements for these experiences in the patient's continuing social network. Then, for each replacement, the patient made a commitment to use the permanent and "real" system, rather than the temporary "treatment" system. During three weeks of inpatient care the patient enlarged his social contacts, starting with role-playing and family counseling group. He joined an ex-patients' group and Alcoholic Anonymous. For a one-year period of followup he has remained abstinent, and reports an enlarged and more satisfying social life.

The process of mourning counseling frequently involves helping a person set up friendship networks to replace the elements of a relationship with therapists. Approaching it as a type of work similar to ordinary mourning work makes clear to all participants that a separation is occurring, and that replacements can be established through focused effort.

Case 3 illustrates a situation in which a problem-solving attitude was newly taken up as a style for approaching domestic disagreements.

A divorced 47-year-old mother of two, usually employed as a legal secretary, was admitted to the Center for a one-month stay following her mother's report that she had crazy beliefs about one of the 1968 Presidential candidates. Soon after admission to an inpatient interval which included phenothiazine medication, the interest in several delusional ideas faded from central attention. Decision counseling started. The patient reported a series of stormy events in her life and marriage; on each occasion, she had left her main place of living to spend increased time with the mother. While with the mother, current "home difficulties" were never discussed. The mother encouraged her "to speak all the ideas in your mind into a telephone" (speaking right over the dial tone). The patient and mother had infrequent contact, usually only in association with such a crisis and usually involving "the speaking out of ideas." In decision counseling, the patient identified the current problem in her life as one not especially difficult, but one which she was not facing. She identified options she had not tried and which seemed promising. She decided that her usual problem response, fleeing the scene to go to her mother and speaking crazy ideas, was unsatisfactory. The decision counselor also convened a few sessions involving the mother and an aunt. The three decided to continue to be available to each other in times of trouble, but to require of each other "a focus on solving real problems." The patient reported that a "jarring but helpful" experience had occurred when the counselor had heard her full range of difficulties, had "decided to remain with her" and did not suggest crazy solutions. The patient is currently employed and is re-entering the life of her two grown children, who report remarkable changes in their mother.

Case 4 illustrates the method in the situation of an adolescent at risk of institutionalization, whose family and network members were convened into the background.

A 15-year-old girl was brought to the Center by the staff of a juvenile court. They were requesting a management opinion regarding a hearing for repeated truancy and also requesting the patient's admission to the Center's adolescent service. The patient, mother and stepfather, during counseling in the home, reviewed their life histories and portrayed a currently turbulent home situation. Frequent moves from place to place had resulted in the patient's having a small social network, and a severe shortage of reading skills. The review was organized around identifying steps which might now improve the social quality of the patient's life, manage the truant relationship with the school and satisfy the concern of the juvenile court. The patient decided to expand reading skills for a planned re-entry to school, attend a summer YMCA day camp and visit her new school to learn its layout and her student responsibilities. With extra reading tutoring, she has finished two semesters of school, with passing grades, and is felt by her teachers to be likely to make it. The school reports to the court have resulted in closure of the case.

SUMMARY   Decision counseling centers upon helping persons-in-crises clarify the cognitive structuring of problems. It can facilitate radical improvement in social and decision skills during an adaptational interval. The method involves an inventory of the problem, of possible responses, design of a decision model and expects competent action. The method can be used in reception, inpatient, outpatient and homecare settings, and is successful with seriously troubled persons. Convening the pertinent members of the family and social network into the effort appears to focus on adaptive action, and reduce the salience of disability and symptoms. Because the method promotes maturation of life-problem skills, it enhances the dignity of individuals and the growth opportunity during adaptational intervals.

REPORT FOUR

INTERRUPTING PROLONGED PATIENTHOOD: AN EXPLORATION OF THE PROBLEMS OF PROVIDING SERVICES TO PROLONGED OR REPEATING USERS WITHOUT UNNECESSARILY CONSTRICTING THEIR OPPORTUNITIES (APRIL 1970)

This fourth report concerns service expected to extend over years as, for instance, might be indicated with schizophrenia. In particular, is it possible to provide such service in non-institutional settings to a group of persons who had experienced much of their previous service within residential institutions?

The pattern of social expectations, for a person in longterm institutional care, may have grown to include a forecast of continuing need for inpatient care, a forecast made with infrequent clinical review. A highly organized day and social system are the central features of a program for returning previously desocialized patients from mental hospitals to productive citizenship.

One-third of a cohort of 66 patients with an average of 14 years previous hospitalization had been converted to outside, independent lives as of an 18-month followup. This patient group was of an age and physical health status compatible with active employment. Measures to reactivate employment skills become, therefore, an aspect of the service design. Patients acquire an interest in life in the non-hospital world as a result of a highly demanding, challenging culture, and conventional, nonpatienthood expectations created within the program.

PREMISES   Long-term patienthood includes a stable role-state marked by (a) infrequent professional review of the patient's current clinical status; (b) infrequent visiting by family; (c) infrequent occurrence of a behavioral or management problem; (d) diminished discussion of "leaving the institution;" and (e) lack of surprise that each new day begins and ends in an institution. Since the time of the events that originally precipitated admission to a mental hospital, much may have changed. The composition of the family unit and its social dynamics may have changed. The job market may be critically different. Because of the multi-year length of many experiences in a mental hospital, the patient may be in a distinctly different part of the life cycle. This infrequent review-of-status helps maintain a rigid persistence of patienthood in an environment which might otherwise offer much potential for surprise and innovation.

BACKGROUND PLANNING   The ten counties of the Rockford Zone contain about 665,000 persons, of which about 800 persons per year go to the state hospitals. The usual hospital discharge patterns prevail. The chances of being discharged diminish dramatically as the length of stay increases. More than nine-tenths of the persons discharged from a state hospital in a given year have been there for less than a year. More than three-quarters of the persons who are in state hospitals on a given day have been there for more than one year. In fact, 52 percent have been there for more than ten years, and 26 percent have been there for more than 20 years.

On an average day in 1964, there were about 1,400 persons from the Rockford Zone territory resident in state hospitals. From study of a sample, we estimated that about half of them were physiologically capable of life outside an institution. On examination, we determined that the primary difficulties that had the effect of prolonging hospitalization were the social breakdown syndrome described by Gruenberg[37] and the institutional desocialization syndrome described by Goffman.[38] Institutional desocialization occurs when the general social environment expresses patienthood-role expectations, and when it assumes, and maintains, life-management functions on behalf of a person. Under such circumstances, an individual's own control systems atrophy. This background suggested that within the institutions historically serving the Rockford Zone territory there might be 700-plus candidates who could be considered for preparation for non-institutional life: they might no longer be acutely disturbed, but would have adopted attitudes and beliefs consistent with institutional life.

CLINICAL METHODS   Appleby's review of resocializing programs[39] finds the active ingredients to be a highly scheduled and organized day, combined with a culture of optimistic, active expectations for return to ordinary, outside life. The most effective daily routine in altering fixed patienthood roles closely duplicates parts of the outside world, and places conventional expectations. Phenothiazine medications are necessary for many in dose levels not greatly affecting alertness[39/40]. Zusman suggests that, in order to establish a continuing non-institutional status, the reduced clarity of the self-concept needs repair, and re-activation of social and job skills for an available job is essential[41].

Ludwig's group describes chronicity-maintaining behaviors used by desocialized persons. These behaviors are used with staff and family, and with anyone attempting to shift the life-style toward life in a non-patienthood social field[42/43]. Desocialized patients counter requests to move to the non-patienthood role system with powerful stabilizing or neutralizing maneuvers: "How can you ask a helpless and confused person to try for such impossible goals?" Ludwig's group describes other methods used by patients to remain inconspicuous, and to avoid the impact of social designs to alter the level of interest in the outside world [42/43].

The Center's Community Return Service works to help individuals return to ordinary communal life after long or frequent hospitalization. Services are based on the premise that continuing contacts may be necessary, but that extramural settings are more desirable, if feasible. It employs a culture of expectations, an active daily routine and a focus on training for employment. Staff and patient attention focuses on daily observable behavior. Throughout the program, the patient is regarded as responsible and accountable for his behavior. Conduct is regularly rated against an explicit set of rules and expectations. During an early intramural phase, levels of ordinary creature comforts are extended in measured amounts only in return for conduct conforming to specified levels of social performance. The expectations placed ask for performance which is close to ordinary and conventional. Conduct distinctly apart from the code is met with amazement, disappointment and even anger by staff and by other patients, in much the way that families and friends might react. Concern for patients is expressed with both tenderness and insistence on competent social performance. Staff focus their attention on observing in the patients that conduct which offers possibilities for opportunities for affection, self-esteem and dignity. Training for employment, along with gradual movement into extramural situations of increasing challenge, are offered on a paced schedule so as to signal a direction and to re-activate latent capacity.

DAILY OPERATIONS   In a 30-bed unit, furnished much like a motel, an average of 24 resident patients, together with 20 formerly resident day patients, lead an active life. A seven-day roster of events provides opportunities for work, socializing and leisure. Work is scheduled for the daytime and study and leisure take place in the evenings. The "planned" style of the day offers an "ordinary" context for the flow of interaction among patients and staff.

    An 8 A.M. consultation establishes continuity between the night and morning staff shifts, develops a planned day for each patient, reviews the patients in outside status and develops the principal clinical management decisions. At 9 A.M. there is a meeting that includes the day staff and all patients. The group assesses several individuals' current behavior, and voices any approval or disapproval it may warrant. A 10:15 A.M. daily, a smaller meeting rates several resident patients, individually, in private sessions. Each week an individual "Resident's Progress Report" is drawn up for each patient[44], which includes discussion of personal, group and communal classes of behaviors. The Report is constructed in close discussion with the patient, and with frequent reference to the Rule Book of the Community Return Service[44]. The "score," and consequent level of privileges, is determined according to the Rules for Five Levels[44]. The five levels entail a detailed specification of privileges and responsibilities, with a gradual release from a tight structure to independence. Lower levels restrict movement, spending money, socializing options and opportunities for solitude. They restrict individual action off-the-unit by allowing certain activities to take place, only in concert with all the other members who are at that level. Thus, patients holding lower level ratings quickly learn to negotiate with the others in that group, because snack-bar visits and other errands require collective action by the group. Meetings by level are scheduled into the day, so that such negotiations may occur. A 2 P.M. session each day offers a variety of special-purpose groups: "Budget planning;" "Moving from level 1 to level 2;" "Exercise;" "Level 3 and 4 shopping;" "Phoning and making appointments;" "Job-hunting information;" "Social opportunities nearby;" etc. At 4 P.M., another meeting draws together the day and evening staff shifts and all resident patients. The Daily Log[44] is read. Events of the working day are evaluated for each patient, using as guidelines the daily plans established in the 8 A.M. meeting. The group voices its assessment of noteworthy behavior. The balance of the planned part of the day includes scheduled sessions for medications review, job training and workshop hours. Unit housekeeping is maintained solely by the patients. Jobs are allocated and rotated regularly. Job-skill workshops for men and women, directed toward earning a living, and for some women, directed toward homemaking, are held in small groups for two hours, five days a week. A Work Rating Sheet[44] is completed with each patient weekly. Work habits, interpersonal relationships in the job-training situation and level of vigor in preparing for socially useful work are used to assess "job readiness."

APPEARANCE OF PATIENTS ON PROGRAM ENTRY   This study covers a cohort of 66 consecutive patierts who entered the program as transfers from state hospitals during a 12-month period beginning July 1, 1967. All patients were selected by the staff of three large mental hospitals on the basis that they could not return usefully to the community in the next year through programs available at that hospital. Additional selection criteria were the following: (1) physiologic status compatible with non-institutional life; (2) age between 17 and 57 years; and (3) absence of ˉevere mental retardation or evidence of gross brain damage.

The 66 patients had experienced an average of 14.2 years of prior hospitalization; 27 had been institutionalized for more than 12 years, and 11 for 25 or more years. At the time of transfer from a large hospital to the program, most patients behaved in a desocialized, chronicity predicting manner. They were dazed, apathetic, slow and inactive. An optimistic note was sounded when some of the patients expressed surprise, amazement and disbelief at the level of preparations that had been made for their entrance, and at the amount of unit routine in which they would be expected to participate.

The age, education, previous social class and job experience suggested a program including training for the unskilled to semi-skilled job market (see Table 7). Of the 66, 44 had never been married; an additional 14 were widowed, divorced or separated. There were 37 men and 29 women in the group.

The 66 patients demonstrated a moderate amount of psychiatric symptoms (see Table 8), with depression, withdrawal, suspicion, and dependency as keynote symptoms. But the staff was impressed that atrophy of social and job skills presented the toughest problems.

Typically, there was no social network beyond the hospital for these patients. Also, they conducted themselves in

Table 7
SELECTED DEMOGRAPHIC CHARACTERISTICS*

Characteristic	Average	Range (N=66)
Age (yr.)	40.9	18–64
Education (yr.)	9.2	4–17
Recent annual income origin family (dollars)	3,300	0–9,000
Childhood socioeconomic status**	V (modal)	I–V

* Patients transferred to the Community Return Service during the 12 months beginning 7/1/69.
** Hollingshead Redlich Two-factor Index of Social Position: I is highest, V is lowest social position origin.

an unattractive and offensive manner not likely to be successful in non-institutional life (see Table 9). Note that many of the problems listed in Table 9 offer little difficulty so long as the patient is hospitalized, and there is no intent to explore discharge possibilities. Most patients experienced at least three or four of the problems enumerated.

Table 8
SYMPTOMS ON TRANSFER*

Symptom Group	No. Patients** (Total 66)	Percent
Depression	32	48
Withdrawal	31	47
Suspicion	25	38
Dependency	25	38
Impulsivity	24	36
Depersonalization, amnesia	23	35
Fighting, tantrums	22	33
Delusional	17	26
Hallucinated	14	21
Alcoholism	6	9
Mute	4	6

* See footnote in Table 7.
** Symptom group counted here when assessed "moderate or severe" on admission mental status examination.

Table 9

MANAGEMENT PROBLEMS ON TRANSFER*

Problem	No. Patients (Total 66)	Percent
No money	62	94
No housing	56	85
No family or equivalent	53	80
No employable skill	48	73
Obviously mentally ill to ordinary citizen	38	58
Considered delinquent by family or court	30	45
Physical disorder needing physician	10	15

* See footnote in Table 7.

RESULTS   The 66 patients spent an average of nine months in the inpatient segment of the project before moving to non-residential extensions, to discharge, or to a return to the state hospital. (Later cohorts have spent only six to seven months.) Table 10 reviews the outcome by level of independence achieved. The assessments of outcome were made two times: in October 1968 (an average of six months after moving to non-residential status), and October 1969 (an average of 18 months after moving to non-residential status, and more than two years after entry into the program).

At the six-month followup point, 27 out of the 66 were independent of the program and of financial supports; while at the 18-month point, 24 were independent (Table 10). Two of the 27 died, one by suicide, and one changed status, needing financial support. Most of the 24 initiate occasional telephone contact with staff, but are not regarded as needing service beyond counseling. Some seek continued contact by note, telephone and "dropping in." Most of the independent group are regarded as likely to remain out of hospitals except for brief episodes. They offer a dramatic contrast to their appearance on transfer into the program after many years of prior hospitalization.

Another group of 16 persons were living outside the hospital but receiving assistance as of the first followup. Some were in a sheltered living or working situation, or both, as for instance, Goodwill Industries. Some were receiving public assistance monies. Others were engaged in job-training programs, but were not independent of support. At the second followup, 14 were in this group, mainly the same persons. Their quality of life was not ideal, but they appraised it as distinctly better than life in the hospital. In any case, they could arrange to go back to the hospital at any time by get-

Table 10
FOLLOWUP STATUS OF 66 CONSECUTIVE PATIENTS*

Level of Independence	July 1967 Status Number	(Percent)	October 1968 Status Number	(Percent)	October 1969 Status Number	(Percent)
Living & working in continuing non-institutional location; no financial support	0		27	41	24	36
Living & working in non-institutional location — receiving some form of financial support	0		16	24	14	21
Usually living outside hospital but requiring crisis support or occasional short admission	0		0		11	17
Still in Community Return Service	0		9	14	1	2
In state hospital	66	100	14	21	14	21
Deceased	0		0		2	3
TOTAL	66	100	66	100	66	100

* Patients entering (transferring in) Community Return Service, 12 months beginning 7/1/67.

ting into such difficulty as would set commitment proceedings into motion. This group also maintained significant contact with program staff. Five were receiving phenothiazine medication.

At the first followup, nine of 66 persons were still in the residential phase of the program. At the second, these nine had moved to a shaky outside status. Mainly, they were living outside the hospital, but occasionally needed several days' hospitalization. Although they were not regarded as successfully resocialized, they were living primarily outside of institutions. Of the original 66, only one was in the residential phase of the program at the second followup. He had been living outside ten months, had briefly returned, and was expected to leave again soon. Staff energy was now increasingly being spent extramurally, much of it in development of more sheltered-care service for the surrounding territory.

There were 14 of 66 people in the state hospital at both followups. They were a different 14. Six of the initial 14 had left the state hospital, while six others entered. Interestingly, the six discharges were by the same staff group which had appraised these patients as non-dischargeable two and one-half years previously. Our information was not complete enough to detect whether the patients were viewed differently or behaved differently.

CASES   Some issues in assessing the quality of the clinical outcomes can be suggested by examining several cases.

Case 1 was an older woman who achieved a good result partly built around beginning a job at a time in life when many are retiring.

A 65-year-old, single, high-school graduate, worked as a successful stenographer for ten years before being hospitalized at age 30 for suspicious and delusional behavior following an illegal abortion. She remained hospitalized for 33 years. Several brief home trials were unsuccessful, as her arguments and delusions quickly frightened her two sisters and precipitated re-hospitalization. At the time of transfer into the program, the patient was taking moderate dosage of chlorpromazine, and talking about a communist plot. On the 96th day of her 155-day stay, the patient was firmly requested, in a group setting, to "stop talking about plots," to join in social activity and to think about some kind of work she would like to do beyond the hospital. There followed a volatile period of greatly increased aggressive talk, crazy at first, but gradually becoming sensible. Concern about plots and manneristic behavior *suddenly* stopped. Over the next 55 days the patient methodically looked for a job. She found a job as a hotel worker, first while living on the unit, then moving out to a shared apartment. She achieved financial independence. Phenothiazine medication was gradually withdrawn during the residential period, and the patient received none on a continuing basis after discharge. She took phenothiazines for an interval of several weeks during several episodes of distress.

In Case 1, and also in Case 2 which follows, there is a point of sudden change in the clinical course. A volatile episode, in the context of a social demand for conventional behavior, is followed by dramatic improvement.

Case 2 also raises issues of deafness and mental retardation.

A 40-year-old deaf-mute had originally been institutionalized in a school for the deaf at the age of four years and he remained there for 12 years. At that time, his intelligence quotient was estimated at 85. At 16 years of age he left the school and lived with his mother until age 34, worked as a polishing-machine operator and carried on a moderate social life. At age 34, when his mother died, the patient started consuming excessive amounts of alcohol, stopped seeing a girl friend, lost a job and entered a mental hospital suffering from depression. During seven years in the hospital, he was regarded as a good bakery worker, offering no critical management problems except episodic headbanging. But on four home-visit trials, he drank alcoholic beverages, did not get a job and returned within a few weeks. He was transferred to the Community Return Service, where he stayed for 400 days. On admission he was alert, but showed deteriorated hygiene and marked inactivity. Intellectual function was assessed using volunteer deaf-mutes. It was discovered that, although the patient seldom used it, he was skilled in sign language. He could also use a quick, shorthand sign language. The volunteer deaf-mutes, and later the patient, taught several staff members this sign language. Through these activities the patient was gradually drawn into group interactions. Coincident with social entry, a volatile week-long interval of disturbance occurred with sleeplessness, headbanging, wall kicking and pacing. In a group setting demands were made, using sign language, to "stop acting crazy and get a job." The volatile disturbance suddenly stopped. The patient established a conventional level of grooming, read the newspaper, found a job in a laundry and moved to an apartment. Fluphenazine enanthate therapy was continued after discharge. The patient lives in a sheltered setting (halfway house) with seven people, but works in an unsheltered situation; he receives a monthly disability pension from the Social Security Administration, but is otherwise self-supporting.

Case 3 reviews a management problem that developed primarily in the period immediately after leaving the residential phase. Several adjustments of the situation have allowed a satisfactory outcome.

A 57-year-old, divorced mother of two was first hospitalized at the age of 25 years following five years of a stormy marriage. The picture than included suspicion and assaultive behavior, and was called paranoid schizophrenia. After 32 years of hospitalization and five unsuccessful trials on home visit, the patient was regarded as no particular problem in residential care but as a poor discharge candidate. She appeared socially inactive and suspicious but maintained ordinary grooming. The patient was transferred to the Community Re-entry Service, where she remained for 96 days. She made rapid early improvement from Level 1 to Level 4. She began to portray herself as a clever and witty woman. She found a job as an attendant in a nursing home. She did well on the job so long as she continued to live on the program unit, but each movement to living alone was accompanied by marked declines in appearance and job function. The patient was closely followed on home visits. Chlorpromazine therapy was continued, and various altered living arrangements were tried. The staff located another female patient of similar social circumstances. Living with her, the patient took hold and has made a new life with an active social network. She is now financially independent, has assumed leadership functions in a social club and is apparently a cherished member of a stable social network. She initiates an infrequent counseling telephone interview with several staff.

COMMENT   More than half the patients in this program either have no family located nearby, or the family is not interested in participation. Arrangements for continuing domicile must, therefore, be independent of the family. Frequently, the arrangements involve other former patients, hotels and rooming houses.

Most observers consider the cohort of 66 patients, as a group, dramatically improved. The average 14 years of prior hospitalization is reflected in the severe picture of desocialization at the time of transfer to the program. Although the average patient in the group became much better off, some did not. One patient died by suicide, and might not have killed himself in an institution. One-third were fully independent at the second followup, but the independent group was smaller (by 3) than a year previously. If this attrition rate continued, all would be back in the hospital by the end of ten years. No further followup of this project has been made to determine the later experience of the group.

About one-fifth of the original 66 patients require external financial support or sheltered living support or both. This group has the same average age and sex composition as the more independent group. We could not have predicted, at the time of transfer into the program, who would move into the higher or lower groups. Both groups are composed almost entirely of schizophrenic persons. The patients with better outcomes do not have a stormier, or quieter, course. They do not have longer, or shorter, average length of prior hospitalization. The staff cannot discern any feature of the clinical picture that will discriminate between the groups except, perhaps, behavior in crisis. Those in the more fortunate group seem a little more able to use advisers in crises. Those in the less fortunate group may send more alienating, more frightening signals to those surrounding them during adaptational intervals.

The one-fifth of the original group who, at the second followup, were outside the hospital but continued to seek relationships with staff and brief re-admissions, are regarded by the staff to be "making it, but more slowly." They may be on a course of gradual re-entry into non-institutional life. At the time of the followups they were in various of "the volatile phases associated with growth." Their average hospitalization prior to transfer to the program is not different than the average for the cohort. But their average length of stay on the residential phase of this program is longer (13 months versus 9 months). During their residential phase they looked worse longer, on the average (but did not reflect a more difficult picture at the worst), than faster patients.

Of the one-fifth who returned to the state hospital, either directly from the community return service or after a period in outside life, about half returned for general medical reasons. They are people of impoverished economic circumstances who have chronic disabilities associated with vision, hearing, seizures, hypertension and diabetes. As an aspect of their situation, they use the state mental hospital for medical or surgical care. Some members of this group might have been able to remain in non-hospital settings if better arrangements could have been established for the supervision of their antipsychotic medications.

An average of 33 persons staff the program for an average 24 inpatients and 20 non-residential, transitional patients. This represents a heavy staff density for public institutions in the late 1960s.

The highly organized daily style in the program may be important as an instrument for stabilizing a culture rapidly and uniformly. Some patients show marked change simply on introduction to the rules-levels-schedule system and to the active, responsible, conventional messages the system carries. The structure provides a ladder upon which interpersonal and group relations can climb. Structure allows conduct to be assessed more objectively and facilitates a focusing of attention on behavior as a whole rather than on symptoms alone.

The crises which occur for a patient during the residential phase are quite dramatic. They often appear as sudden, quite visible, clinical turning points (see cases 1, 2 and 3). The special flexibility of the crisis or adaptational state is discussed by many workers[45], but Propst makes the particular point that many longterm mental patients, stabilized at a level of marked social disability, have a dramatic reduction in symptoms following a performance demand coupled with such a crisis.[46] It is as if a stable state sometimes cannot be relinquished without a critical event and period of special volatility. The staff has learned to hesitate from heavily medicating patients during the volatile interval but, instead, to supply increased interpersonal contact and unremitting demands for growth. They also avoid labeling these volatile intervals as "illness" or "regression;" they refer to them as "special transition times" and imply an optimistic stage and sequence is in process. An administrative structure has been placed around the use of "confrontation events." The senior administrator clinically provides a professional model through his handling of the method. Any challenges to patients may only be given in group settings with prior staff discussion. Meetings of the staff are regularly convened to review relationships between methods and goals. The Daily Log[44] must record the event, with an associated record of the group critique of the event. This method requires simultaneous encounters with intense belief and with scientific reflection about productivity.

The practices that link levels of privilege with levels of performance seem to accelerate change. This may be because movement to personally desired objectives is coupled with fulfillment of social role expectations, a model loosely congruent with the usual social world. Just as important, very small amounts of clinical change can be meaningfully discussed by staff and patients. Since there is not the fast patient movement in this program that might be found in some other settings, a more finely calibrated scheme for assessing change better fits the situation.

The collective impact of having available an adequate number of several types of shelter-care and shelter-work settings emerges as an active principle in this program[46,47]. Several community agencies are developing more sheltered settings in the program's territory, apparently in response to the recently increased flow of persons in post-institutional status.

The treatment elements of collective belief, structured routine, graded privilege and training for employment, are in no sense new, even as a combination. Ruth Caplan[48] has identified the presence of these elements intermittently in American psychiatry several times since 1800. For instance, the "tent treatment" for chronically institutionalized persons was demonstrated by Arthur Wright[49] at Manhattan State Hospital, East (Ward's Island, New York) in 1901 to be an effective health-promoting method. The "tent treatment" refers to a situation which surprised contemporary officials in 1900 and 1901 when a large number of aged and chronically ill persons suddenly improved when they were removed from a large, overcrowded hospital building and placed in bivouac tents around the Island while the usual facility was being repaired. Many were so distinctly improved that they or their families requested their discharge. An active discussion ensued concerning the identification of the active ingredient in the very powerful "tent treatment." Wilsey, in 1903, in a closely reasoned discussion,[50] argued that a changed life environment, one with opportunity for roles in a group, was the important agent. But, in practice, the active elements were misidentified as illumination and ventilation and the method was lost.

References

CHAPTER II

1. Bruner, J. S. *On knowing: essays for the left hand.* Cambridge: Harvard University Press, 1962.
2. Darwin, C. *The expression of the emotions in man and animals.* Chicago: University of Chicago Press, 1965 (original, 1872).
3. Erikson, E. *Identity and the life cycle.* New York: International Universities Press, 1964.
4. Freud, S. *An outline of psychoanalysis.* New York: Norton, 1949.
5. Piaget, J. *The construction of reality in the child.* New York: Basic Books, 1954.
6. Piaget, J. *The mechanisms of perception.* New York: Basic Books, 1969.
7. Skinner, B. F. *Science and human behavior.* New York: Macmillan, 1953.
8. Pribam, K. H. *Languages of the brain.* Englewood Cliffs, N.J.: Prentice-Hall, 1971.
9. Wallace, A. F. C. *Culture and personality.* New York: Random House, 1961.

CHAPTER III

1. Richter, C. P. The behavioral regulation of homeostasis. *Symposium on Stress.* Washington, D.C.: Walter Reed Army Medical Center, 1953, 78-88.
2. Cannon, W. B. *The wisdom of the body.* New York: Norton, 1932.
3. Selye, H. *Stress.* Montreal: Acta Medical Publishers, 1950.
4. Bowlby, J. Separation anxiety. *Int J Psycho-Anal,* 1960, **41:**1-25 (Parts 1-2).

5. Bowlby, J. The processes of mourning. *Int J Psycho-Anal*, 1961, **42:**317-340 (Parts 4-5).
6. Lindemann, E. Symptomatology and management of acute grief. *Amer J Psychiat*, September, 1944, **101:**141-148.
7. Visotsky, H. M., Hamburg, D. A., Goss,M. E., Lebovitts, B. Z. Coping behavior under extreme stress. *Arch Gen Psychiat*, November 1961, **5:**423-448.
8. Coelho, G. V., Hamburg, D. A., Murphy, E. B. Coping strategies in a new learning environment. *Arch Gen Psychiat*, November 1963, **9:**433-443.
9. Wallace, A. F. C. Mazeway distingegration: the individual's perception of socio-cultural disorganization. *Hum Org*, Summer 1957, **16:**23-27.
10. Sims, J. H. & Bauman, D. D. The tornado threat: coping styles of the north and south. *Science*, 30 June 1972, **176:**1386-1392.
11. Tyhurst, J. S. The role of transition states—including disasters—in mental illness. *Symposium on Social and Preventive Psychiatry*. Washington, D. C.: Walter Reed Army Institute of Research (WRAIR), 1957, 149-172.
12. Caplan, G. Patterns of parental response to the crisis of premature birth. *Psychiat*, November 1960, **23:**365-374.
13. Pribam, K. H. Feelings as monitors. In M. B. Arnold (Ed.), *Feelings and emotions*. New York: Academic Press, 1970, 41-53.
14. Scheflen, A. E. Human communication: behavioral programs and their integration in interaction. *Behav Sci*, January 1968, **13:**44-55.
15. Silber, E., Hamburg, D. A., Coelho, G. V., Murphey, E. B., Rosenberg, M. & Pearlin, L. I. Adaptive behavior in competent adolescents. *Arch Gen Psychiat*, October 1961, **5:**354-365.
16. Siber, E., Coelho, G. V., Murphey, E. B., Hamburg, D. A., Pearlin, L. I. & Rosenberg, M. Competent adolescents coping with college decisions. *Arch Gen Psychiat*, December 1961, **5:**517-527.
17. Fitzgerald, R. S. Reactions to blindness. *Arch Gen Psychiat*, April 1970, **22:**370-379.

18. Melges, F. T. & Bowlby, J. Types of hopelessness in psychopathologic process. *Arch Gen Psychiat,* June 1969, **20:**690-699.
19. Pribam, K. H. *Languages of the brain.* Englewood Cliffs, N.J.: Prentice-Hall, 1971, especially 99-115, 167-214 and 252-270.
20. Selye, H. The general adaptation syndrome and diseases of adaptation. *J Clin Endocrinol,* February 1946, **6:**217-230.
21. Hinkle, L. E., Plummer, N., Metraux, R., Richter, P., Gittinger, J. W., Thetford, W. N., Ostfeld, A. M., Kane, F. D., Goldberger, L., Mitchell, W. E., Leichter, H., Pinsky, R., Goebel, D., Bross, I. D. J. & Wolff, H. G. Studies in human ecology. *Amer J Psychiat,* September 1957, **114:**212-220.
22. Rahe, R. H., McKean, J. D., Jr., & Arthur, R. J. A longitudinal study of life-change and illness patterns. *J Psychosom Res,* 1967, **10:**355-366.
23. Wyler, A. R., Masuda, M. & Holmes, T. H. Magnitude of life events and seriousness of illness. *Psychosom Med,* March-April 1971, **33:**115-122.

CHAPTER IV

1. Bazelon, D. Remarks of the court, T. H. Washington v. U. S. A., D. C. Circuit No. 20232, December 13, 1967. Washington, D. C.: Administrative Office, U. S. Courts, 1967.
2. American Psychiatric Association. *Diagnostic and statistical manual of mental disorders.* (2nd ed.) Washington, D. C.: American Psychiatric Association, 1968.
3. Spitzer, R. L. & Endicott, J. Diagno II: Further developments in a computer program for psychiatric diagnosis. *Amer J Psychiat,* January 1969, **125:**12-21.
4. Rubin, B. Prediction of dangerousness in mentally ill criminals. *Arch Gen Psychiat,* September 1972, **27:**397-467.
5. Appel, J. W. Preventive psychiatry. In R. S. Anderson,

A. J. Glass & R. J. Bernucci (Eds.), *Neuropsychiatry in World War II.* Vol. 1: Zone of the interior. Washington D. C.: Department of the Army, 1966, 373-415, especially pp. 389 ff.

6. Gurland, B. J., Fleiss, J. L., Cooper, J. E., Sharpe, L., Kendell, R. E., & Roberts, P. Cross-national study of mental disorders: hospital diagnosis and hospital patients in New York and London. *Comprehens Psychiat,* January 1970, **11:**18-25.

7. Srole, L., Langner, T. S., Michael, S. T., Opler, M. K., & Rennie, T. A. C. *Mental health in the metropolis.* New York: McGraw-Hill, 1962. (Parts of this work are abstracted in *Internat J Psychiat,* 1964, **1:**64-75.

8. Kramer, H. & Sprenger, J. *Malleus maleficarum.* Translated with introduction, notes and bibliography by M. Summers. London: John Rodker, 1928 (from first edition, Cologne, 1489).

9. Kupfer, D. J., Wyatt, R. J., Scott, J. & Snyder, F. Sleep disturbance in acute schizophrenic patients. *Amer J Psychiat,* March 1970, **126:**1213-1223.

10. Gaardner, K. A conceptual model of sleep. *Arch Gen Psychiat,* March 1966, **14:**253-260.

11. Hinkle, Jr., L. E., & Wolff, H. G. The methods of interrogation and indoctrination used by the communist state police. *Bull NY Acad Med,* 1957, **33:**600-622.

12. Sargeant, W. *Battle for the mind.* New York: Doubleday, 1957.

13. Glass, A. J. Observations upon the epidemiology of mental illness in troops during warfare. *Symposium on Social and Preventive Psychiatry.* Washington, D. C.: Walter Reed Army Institute of Research (WRAIR), 1957, 185-198.

14. Rosenthal, S. H. Electrosleep: a double-blind clinical study. *Biol Psychiat,* 1972, **4:**179-189.

15. Kupfer, D. J., Wyatt, R. J., Snyder, F. & Davis, J. Chlorpromazine and sleep in psychiatric patients. *Arch Gen Psychiat,* February 1971, **24:**185-189.

16. Kety, S. S. Toward hypotheses for a biochemical component in the vulnerability to schizophrenia. *Sem Psychiat,* August 1972, **4**:233-238.

17. Kety, S. S., Rosenthal, D., Wender, P. H., & Schulsinger, F. et al. The types and prevalence of mental illness in the biological and adoptive families of adopted schizophrenics. *J Psychiat Res,* 1968, **6**(suppl #1):345-366.

18. Heston, L. L. The genetics of schizophrenic and schizoid disease. *Science,* 1970, **167**:249-256.

19. Heston, L. L. Psychiatric disorders in foster home reared children of schizophrenic mothers. *Brit J Psychiat,* 1966, **112**:819-825.

20. Hoffer, A. & Pollin, W. Schizophrenia in the NAS-NRC panel of 15,909 veteran twin pairs. *Arch Gen Psychiat,* November 1970, **23**:469-477.

21. Axelrod, J., Mueller, R. A., Henry, J. P. & Stephens, P. M. Changes in enzymes involved in the biosynthesis and metabolism of noradrenaline and adrenaline after psychosocial stimulation. *Nature,* 14 March 1971, **225**:1059-1060.

22. Axelrod, J. Noradrenaline: fate and control of its biosynthesis. *Science,* 13 August 1971, **173**:598-606.

23. Axelrod, J. Biogenic amines and their impact in psychiatry. *Sem Psychiat,* August 1972, **4**:199-210.

24. Stein, L. & Wise, E. D. Possible etiology of schizophrenia: progressive damage to the noradrenergic reward system by b-hydroxydopamine. *Science,* 12 March 1971, **171**:1132-1136.

25. NIMH-Psychopharmacology Service Center Collaborative Study Group. Phenothiazine treatment in acute schizophrenia. *Arch Gen Psychiat,* March 1964, **10**:246-261.

26. Bleuler, M. Some results of research in schizophrenia. *Behav Sci,* May 1970, **15**:211-219.

27. Gruenberg, E. M. & Huxley, J. Mental health services can be organized to prevent chronic disability. *Commun Ment Health J,* 1970, **6**:431-436.

28. Gruenberg, E. M. From practice to theory: community mental health services and the nature of psychoses. *The Lancet,* 5 April 1969, 721-724.
29. Gruenberg, E. M. The social breakdown syndrome—some origins. *Amer J Psychiat,* June 1967, **123:**1481-1489.
30. Pasamanick, B., Scarpitti, F. R. & Dinitz, S. *Schizophrenics in the community. An experimental study in the prevention of hospitalization.* New York: Appleton-Century-Crofts, 1967, especially pp. 99-166.
31. Kramer, M. Epidemiology, biostatistics, and mental health planning. In R. M. Monroe, R. R. Monroe, G. D. Klee, & E. B. Brody, (Eds.), *Psychiatric epidemiology and mental health planning* (American Psychiatric Res Rep # 22). Washington, D. C.: American Psychiatric Association, 1967, 1-63.
32. Kramer, M. *Applications of mental health statistics.* Geneva: World Health Organization, 1969.
33. Kramer, M. *Some implications of trends in the usage of psychiatric facilities for community mental health programs and related research* (PHS Publication #1434). Washington, D. C.: U. S. Department of Health, Education and Welfare, 1967.
34. Kramer, M., Taube, C., & Starr, S. Patterns of use of psychiatric facilities by the aged: current status, trends, and implications. In A. Simon & L. J. Epstein, (Eds.), *Aging in modern society* (Psychiat Res Rep #23). Washington, D. C.: American Psychiatric Association, 1968, 89-150.
35. National Center for Health Statistics. *Socioeconomic characteristics of diseased persons, U. S., 1962-63 Deaths* (Serial 22, #9). Washington, D. C.: U. S. Department of Health, Education and Welfare, 1969.
36. Malzberg, B. Mental disease among the native and foreign-born white population of New York State, 1939-1941. *Ment Hyg,* 1955, **39:**545-559.
37. Malzberg, B. Rates of mental disease among certain categories of population groups in New York State. *J Amer Stat Assoc,* 1936, **31:**545-548.

38. Visotsky, H. M., Hamburg, D. A., Goss, M. E. & Le-
    bovitts, B. Z. Coping behavior under extreme stress.
    Arch Gen Psychiat, 1961, **5:**423-448.
39. Rubin, B. & Eisen, S. B. The old timers' club. *Arch Neurol
    and Psychiat,* January 1958, **79:**113-121.
40. Caplan, R. *Psychiatry and the community in nineteenth-
    century America.* New York: Basic Books, 1969, Chapter
    26.
41. Wright, A. B. Tent life for the demented and uncleanly.
    Amer J Insan, 1902, **59:**315-319.
42. Wilsey, O. J. Tent life for the insane. *Amer J Insan,* 1903,
    59:629-635.
43. Henry, J. P., Stephens, P. M., Axelrod, J. & Mueller, R. A.
    Effect of psychosocial stimulation on the enzymes in-
    volved in the biosynthesis and metabolism of noradren-
    aline and adrenaline. *Psychosom Med,* May-June 1971,
    33:227-237.
44. Kramer, M. A discussion of the concepts of incidence
    and prevalence as related to epidemiologic studies of
    mental disorders. *Amer J Publ Health,* July 1957, **47:**
    826-840.
45. Kramer, M. Long range studies of mental hospital pa-
    tients. *Milbank Mem Fund Quart,* July 1953, **31:**253-264.
46. Kramer, M., Goldstein, H., Israel, R. H., & Johnson, N. A.
    *Dispositions of first admissions to a state mental hospi-
    tal* (Public Health Service Publication #445.) Washing-
    ton, D. C.: U. S. Department of Health, Education and
    Welfare/PHS, 1955.
47. Hansell, N. & Benson, M. L. Interrupting long-term pa-
    tienthood. *Arch Gen Psychiat,* March 1971, **24:**238-243.
48. Zusman, J. Some explanations of the changing appear-
    ance of psychotic patients. In E. M. Gruenberg, (Ed.),
    *Evaluating the effectiveness of community mental
    health services.* New York: Milbank, 1966, 363-394.
49. Rowitz, L. & Levy, L. Ecological analysis of treated men-
    tal disorders in Chicago. *Arch Gen Psychiat,* November
    1968, **19:**571-579.

50. Levy, L. & Rowitz, L. Ecological attributes of high and low rate mental hospital utilization areas in Chicago. *Soc Psychiat*, January 1971, **6**:20-28.
51. Levy, L. & Rowitz, L. The spatial distribution of treated mental disorders in Chicago. *Soc Psychiat*, 1970, **5**:1-11.
52. Temoche, A., Pugh, T. F. & MacMahon, B. Suicide rates among current and former mental institution patients. *J Nerv Ment Dis*, February 1964, **138**:124-130.
53. McInnes, R. S., Palmer, J. T. & Downing, J. J. An analysis of the service relationships between state mental hospitals and one local mental health program. *California Department of Mental Hygiene Biostatistics* (Bulletin 23). Sacramento: State of California, 1962.
54. Stubblebine, J. M. & Decker, J. B. Are urban mental health centers worth it? (Part 2) *Amer J Psychiat*, October 1971, **128**:480-483.
55. Decker, J. B. & Stubblebine, J. M. Crisis intervention and prevention of psychiatric disability: a follow-up study. *Amer J Psychiat*, December 1972, **129**:725-729.
56. Brenner, M. H. Economic change and mental hospitalization: New York State, 1910-1960. *Soc Psychiat*, 1967, **2**:180-188.
57. Ludwig, A. M. & Farrelly, F. The code of chronicity. *Arch Gen Psychiat*, December 1966, **15**:562-568.
58. Ludwig, A. M. & Farrelly, F. The weapons of insanity. *Amer J Psychother*, October 1967, **21**:737-749.

CHAPTER V

1. Ryan, W. Distress in the city. *A summary report of the Boston mental health survey*. Boston: United Community Services of Metropolitan Boston, 1964.
2. Mechanic, D. & Volkart, E. H. Stress, illness behavior, and the sick role. *Amer Sociolog Rev*, 1961, **26**:51-58.
3. Parsons, T. Illness and the role of the physician. *Amer J Orthopsychiat*, 1951, **21**:452-460.
4. Scheff, T. B. *Being mentally ill*. Chicago: Aldine, 1966.
5. Simmons, O. G. & Freeman, H. E. Familial expectations

and post-hospital performance of mental patients. *Human Relat*, August 1959, **21**:233-241.

6. Sarbin, T. R. Notes on the transformation of social identity. In Roberts, L. M., Greenfield, N. S., & Miller, M. H., (Eds.), *Comprehensive mental health: the challenge of evaluation*. Madison: University of Wisconsin Press, 1968, 97-115.

7. Parad, H. J. & Caplan, G. A framework for studying families in crisis. *J Soc Work*, 1960, **5**:3-15.

8. Caplan, G. Beyond the child guidance clinic. Paper presented at the twenty-fifth anniversary celebration of the New Orleans Mental Hygiene Foundation, New Orleans, January 28, 1964.

9. Caplan, G. *Principles of preventive psychiatry*. New York: Basic Books, 1964, 26-55.

10. Caplan, R. *Helping the helpers to help*. New York: Seabury, 1972, 16-36.

11. Adler, H. M. & Hammett, V. B. O. Crisis, conversion and cult formation. *Amer J Psychiat*, August 1973, **130:** 861-864.

12. Bergman, R. L. A school for medicine men. *Amer J Psychiat*, June 1973, **130**:663-669.

13. Torrey, E. F. Who says witch doctors aren't relevant? *Hospital Physician*, 1971, **5**:122-127.

14. Torrey, E. F. The case for the indigenous therapist. *Arch Gen Psychiat*, 1969, **30**:365-373.

15. Hinkle, L. E. Ecological observations of the relation of physical illness, mental illness and the social environment. *Psychosom Med*, July-August 1961, **23**:289-297.

16. Hinkle, L. E. & Wolff, H. G. Ecologic investigations of the relationship between illness, life experiences and the social environment. *Ann Int Med*, December 1958, **49**:1373-1388.

17. Hinkle, L. E., Plummer, N., Metraux, R., Richter, P., Gittinger, J. W., Thetford, W. N., Ostfeld, A. M., Kane, F. D., Goldberger, L., Mitchell, W. E., Leichter, H., Pinsky, R., Goebel, D., Brose, I. D. J., & Wolff, H. G. Studies in human ecology. *Amer J. Psychiat*, September 1957, **114**:212-220.

18. Miller, G. A. Communication and information as limiting factors in group formation. *Symposium on preventive and social psychiatry.* Washington, D. C.: Walter Reed Army Institute of Research (WRAIR), 1957, 1-15.
19. Coleman, M. D. & Zwerling, I. The psychiatric emergency clinic: a flexible way of meeting community mental health needs. *Amer J Psychiat,* 1959, **115**:980-984.
20. Strickler, M., Bassin, E. G., Malbin, V., & Jacobson, G. F. The community-based walk-in center: a new resource for groups underrepresented in out-patient treatment facilities. *Amer J Publ Health,* March 1965, **55**:377-384.
21. Lion, J. R., Bach-Y-Rita, G., & Ervin, F. R. Violent patients in the emergency room. *Amer J Psychiat,* June 1969, **125**:1706-1711.
22. Spivak, G., Schwartz, S., Goldman, C., & Prewitt, J. Symptom syndromes of emergency cases in an urban community mental health center. *Compreh Psychiat,* May 1972, **13**:265-273.
23. Schwartz, D. A., Weiss, A. T., & Miner, J. M. Community psychiatry and emergency service. *Amer J Psychiat,* December 1972, **129**:710-715.
24. Galdston, R. & Hughes, M. C. Pediatric hospitalization as crisis intervention. *Amer J Psychiat,* December 1972, **129**:721-725.
25. Querido, A. The shaping of community mental health care. *Brit J Psychiat,* March 1968, **114**:293-302.
26. Torrey, E. F. Emergency psychiatric ambulance services in the USSR. *Amer J Psychiat,* August 1971, **128**: 153-157.
27. Kirkbride, T. S. Construction, organization and general arrangements of hospitals for the insane. *Amer J Insan,* 1854, **11**:1-37 and 122-163. (Excerpts reprinted in *Mental Hospitals,* 1955, **6**:14-20.)
28. Kirkbride, T. S. Description of the pleasure grounds and farm of the Pennsylvania hospital for the insane. *Amer J Insan,* April 1848, **4**:347-354.
29. Ludwig, A. M. & Farrelly, F. The code of chronicity. *Arch Gen Psychiat,* December 1966, **15**:562-568.

30. Ludwig, A. M. & Farrelly, F. The weapons of insanity. *Amer J Psychother,* October 1967, **21:**737-749.
31. Hansell, N. & Benson, M. L. Interrupting prolonged patienthood. *Arch Gen Psychiat,* March 1971, **24:**238-243.
32. Stubblebine, J. M. & Decker, J. B. Are urban mental health centers worth it? *Amer J Psychiat,* 1971, **127:** 908-912.
33. Stubblebine, J. M. & Decker, J. B. Are urban mental health centers worth it? (Part II) *Amer J Psychiat,* October 1971, **128:**480-483.
34. Decker, J. B. & Stubblebine, J. M. Crisis intervention and prevention of psychiatric disability: a follow-up study. *Amer J Psychiat,* Ocotber 1972, **129:**725-729.'
35. McInnes, R. S. Palmer, J. T., & Downing, J. J. An analysis of the service relationships between state mental hospitals and one local mental health program. *California Department of Mental Hygiene Biostatistics (Bulletin 23).* Sacramento: State of California, 1962.
36. Epstein, L. J. & Simon, A. Alternatives to state hospitalization for the geriatric mentally ill. *Amer J Psychiat,* 1968, **124:**955-961.
37. Hansell, N. A system: patient predicament and clinical service. *Arch Gen Psychiat,* August 1967, **17:**204-210.
38. Gruenberg, E. M. & Huxley, J. Mental health services can be organized to prevent chronic disability. *Commun Ment Health J,* 1970, **6:**431-436.
39. Langsley, D. S., Machotka, P. & Flomanhaft, K. Avoiding mental hospital admission: a follow-up study. *Amer J Psychiat,* April 1971, **127:**1371-1382.
40. Hertz, M. I., Endicott, J., Spitzer, R. C. & Mesnikoff, A. Day versus inpatient hospitalization: a controlled study. *Amer J Psychiat,* April 1971, **127:**1371-1382.
41. Pasamanick, B., Scarpitti, F. R. & Dinitz, S. Schizophrenics in the community. In Dinitz, S., Dynes, B. B., and Clarke, A. C., (Eds.), *Deviance: studies in the process of stigmatization and societal reaction.* New York: Oxford University Press, 1969, 516-523.
42. Hansell, N. Elements of a local service system. In G. Cap-

lan, Ed. *Child and adolescent psychiatry, sociocultural and community psychiatry* (Volume II, S. Arieti (Ed.). *American handbook of psychiatry*, second edition.) New York: Basic Books, 1974.

CHAPTER VI

1. Dix, D. L. Memorial to the legislature of Massachusetts (1843). Reprinted in B. Blatt (Ed.), *Exodus from pandemonium.* Boston: Allyn & Bacon, 1970, 31-56.
2. Caplan, R. B. *Psychiatry and the community in nineteenth-century America.* New York: Basic Books, 1969, especially 3-97.
3. Rothman, D. J. *The discovery of asylum.* Boston: Little-Brown, 1971.
4. Kirkbride, T. S. Description of the pleasure grounds and farm of the Pennsylvania hospital for the insane. *Amer J Insan,* April 1848, **4:**347-354.
5. Kirkbride, T. S. Construction, organization and general arrangements of hospitals for the insane. *Amer J Insan,* 1854, **11:**1-37 and 122-163. (Excerpts reprinted in *Mental Hospital,* 1955, **6:**14-20.)
6. Standing Committee, Association of Medical Superintendents of American Institutions for the Insane. Report on the construction of hospitals for the insane. *Amer J Insan,* July 1851, **8:**74-76.
7. Channing, W. Remarks on the address of St. Weir Mitchell. *Amer J Insan,* 1894, **51:**171-181.
8. Jones, M. *The therapeutic community.* New York: Basic Books, 1953.
9. Stanton, A. H. & Schwartz, M. S. *The mental hospital.* New York: Basic Books, 1954.
10. Goffman, E. *Asylums.* New York: Doubleday, 1961.
11. Rubin, B. & Goldberg, A. An investigation of openness in the psychiatric hospital. *Arch Gen Psychiat,* March 1963, **8:**269-276.
12. Rubin, B. & Eisen, S. B. The old timers' club. *Arch Neurol & Psychiat,* January 1958, **79:**113-121.

13. Kramer, M. Collection and utilization of statistical data from psychiatric facilities in the United States of America. *Bull World Health Org,* 1963, **29:**491-510.

14. U. S. Department of Health, Education and Welfare, Public Health Service, Biometrics Branch. Unpublished data obtained from 11 of the states in the model repeating area for mental health statistics, 1964.

15. Kramer, M. *Some implications of trends in the usage of psychiatric facilities community mental health programs and related research.* (PHS Publication #1434.) Washington, D. C.: U. S. Department of Health, Education and Welfare, 1966. (See, for instance, the gradual flattening of the slope in Figures 10a, 10b, 12a, 13a and 14a.)

16. Kramer, M., Goldstein, H., Israel, R. H., & Johnson, N. A. *Disposition of first admissions to a state mental hospital.* (Public Health Service Publ #445.) Washington, D. C.: U. S. Department of Health, Education and Welfare/PHS, 1955. (See, for example, Table 5.)

17. Langsley, D. S., Machotka, P. & Flomanhaft, K. Avoiding mental hospital admission: a follow-up study. *Amer J Psychiat,* April 1971, **127:**1391-1394.

18. Hertz, M. I., Endicott, J., Spitzer, R. C. & Mesnikoff, A. Day versus inpatient hospitalization: a controlled study. *Amer J Psychiat,* April 1971, **127:**1371-1382.

19. Temoche, A., Pugh, T. F. & MacMahon, B. Suicide rates among current and former mental institution patients. *J New Ment Dis,* February 1964, **138:**124-130.

20. Hansell, N. & Visotsky, H. M. Trends within psychiatry during the 1950's and 1960's. *World Medical News* (supplement), October 1969. (This article used otherwise unpublished data supplied by Biometrics Section, National Institute of Mental Health, September 1969.)

21. Kellam, S. G., Shmelzer, J. L. & Berman, A. Variation in the atmospheres of psychiatric wards. *Arch Gen Psychiat,* June 1966, **14:**561-570.

22. Rosenham, D. L. On being sane in insane places. *Science,* 19 January 1973, **179:**250-258.

23. Ludwig, A. M. & Farrelly, F. The code of chronicity. *Arch Gen Psychiat,* December 1966, **15**:562-568.
24. Ludwig, A. M. & Farrelly, F. The weapons of insanity. *Amer J Psychother,* October 1967, **21**:737-749.
25. Ludwig, A. M. The influence of non-specific healing techniques with chronic schizophrenics. *Amer J Psychother,* July 1968, **22**:382-404.
26. Ludwig, A. M. Chronic schizophrenia: clinical and therapeutic issues. *Amer J Psychother,* July 1970, **24**:380-399.
27. Hansell, N. & Benson, M. L. Interrupting prolonged patienthood. *Arch Gen Psychiat,* March 1971, **24**:238-243.
28. Wing, J. K. & Brown, G. W. *Institutionalism and schizophrenia: a comparative study of three mental hospitals, 1960-1968.* Cambridge (England): Cambridge University Press, 1970.
29. Jackson, G. W. & Smith, F. V. The Kansas plan. *Ment Hosp,* January 1961, **12**:5-8.
30. U. S. Department of Health, Education and Welfare. Regulations for the community mental health centers act of 1963. In *Federal Register.* Washington, D. C.: U. S. Government Printing Office, May 6, 1964, 5951-5956.
31. LaFave, H. G., Stewart, A. & Grunberg, F. Community care of the mentally ill: implementation of the Saskatchewan plan. *Commun Ment Health,* February 1968, **4**:37-45.
32. Gruenberg, E. M. & Huxley, J. Mental health services can be organized to prevent chronic disability. *Commun Ment Health J,* 1970, **6**:431-436.
33. Stubblebine, M. & Decker, J. B. Are urban mental health centers worth it? *Amer J Psychiat,* January 1971, **127**:908-912.
34. Stubblebine, J. M. & Decker, J. B. Are urban mental health centers worth it? (Part II) *Amer J Psychiat,* October 1971, **128**:480-483.
35. Kramer, M. Epidemiology, biostatistics, and mental health planning. In R. R. Monroe, G. D. Klee & E. B. Brody, (Eds.), *Psychiatric epidemiology and mental health planning.* (American Psychiatric Association Re-

search Report #22.) Washington, D. C.: American Psychiatric Association, 1967, 1-63.

36. Kramer, M., Taube, C., & Starr, S. Patterns of use of psychiatric facilities by the aged: current status, trends, and implications. In A. Simon & L. J. Epstein (Eds.), *Aging in modern society*. (American Psychiatric Association Research Report #23). Washington, D. C.: American Psychiatric Association, 1968, 89-150.

37. National Center for Health Statistics. Socioeconomic characteristics of diseased persons, U. S., 1962-63 deaths. (Serial 22 #9) Washington, D. C.: U. S. Department of Health, Education and Welfare, 1969.

38. Malzberg, B. Mental disease among the native and foreign-born white populations of New York State, 1939-1941. *Ment Hyg*, 1945, **39**:545-559.

39. Malzberg, B. Rates of mental disease among certain categories of population groups in New York State. *J Amer Stat Assoc*, 1936, **31**:545-548.

40. Landy, D. & Greenblatt, M. *Halfway house: a sociocultural and clinical study of Rutland Corner House, a transitional aftercare residence for female psychiatric patients*. Washington, D. C.: Vocational Rehabilitation Administration, 1965.

41. Fairweather, S. W., Sanders, D. H., Maynard, H. & Cressler, D. L. *Community life for the mentally ill: an alternative to institutional care*. Chicago: Aldine, 1969.

42. Gross, H. J. Self-help through recovery, Inc. In J. H. Masserman (Ed.), *Current psychiatric therapies*. Vol. 11. New York: Grune and Stratton, 1971, 156-160.

43. Zurcher, L. A. & Green, A. E. *From dependency to dignity: individual and social consequences of a neighborhood house*. New York: Behavioral Publications, 1969.

44. Hobbs, N. Helping disturbed children: psychological and ecological strategies. *Amer Psychol*, December 1966, **21**:1105-1115.

45. Wechsler, H. The self-help organization in the mental health field. *J Nerv Ment Dis*, 1960, **130**:297-314.

46. U. S. Census of Population, 1960. *Persons by family*

characteristics. (Series PC (2)-4B.) Washington, D. C.: Bureau of Census, 1960. (Table 2, cited in Kramer, *op. cit.*, 1967.)

47. Caplan, R. *Psychiatry and the community in nineteenth-century America.* New York: Basic Books, 1969, Chapter 26.

48. Wright, A. B. Tent life for the demented and uncleanly. *Amer J Insan*, 1902, **59:**315-319.

49. Wilsey, O. J. Tent life for the insane. *Amer J Insan*, 1903, **60:**629-635.

50. Hansell, N. *Manual of the spin-off group method.* Chicago: Northwestern University Medical School, 1969.

51. Hansell, N. Elements of a local service system. In G. Caplan (Ed.). *Child and adolescent psychiatry, sociocultural and community psychiatry* (Volume II, S. Arieti, (Ed.). *American handbook of psychiatry*, second edition, in six volumes). New York: Basic Books, 1974.

52. Axelrod, J. Noradrenaline: fate and control of its biosynthesis. *Science*, 13 August 1971, **173:**598-606.

53. Axelrod, J. Biogenic amines and their impact in psychiatry. *Sem Psychiat*, August 1972, **4:**199-210.

54. Kety, S. S. Toward hypotheses for a biochemical component in the vulnerability to schizophrenia. *Sem Psychiat*, August 1972 **4:**233-338.

55. Snyder, S. H. Catecholamines in the brain as mediators of amphetamine psychosis. *Arch Gen Psychiat*, August 1972, **27:**169-179.

56. Snyder, S. H. Amphetamine psychosis: a "model" schizophrenia mediated by catecholamines. *Amer J Psychiat*, January 1973, **130:**61-67.

57. NIMH-Psychopharmacology Service Center Collaborative Study Group. Phenothiazine treatment in acute schizophrenia. *Arch Gen Psychiat*, March 1964, **10:**246-261.

58. Pasamanick, B., Scarpitti, F. R., Lefton, M., Dinitz, S., Wernert, J. J. & McPheeters, H. Home vs hospital care for schizophrenics. *J Amer Med Assoc*, 1964, **187:**177-181.

59. Mendel, W. M. Effect of length of hospitalization on rate

and quality of remission from acute psychotic episodes. *J New Ment Dis*, 1966, **143**:226-233.

60. NIMH-Psychopharmacology Service Center Collaborative Study Group. Phenothiazine treatment in acute schizophrenia. *Arch Gen Psychiat*, March 1964, **10**:246-261.

61. Hogarty, G. E. Goldberg, S. C. & Collaborative Study Group. Drug and sociotherapy in the aftercare of schizophrenic patients. *Arch Gen Psychiat*, January 1973, **28**:54-64.

CHAPTER VII

REPORT ONE

1. von Bertalanffy, L. An outline of general system theory. *Brit J Phil Sci*, 1950, **1**:134-159.

2. von Bertalanffy, L. The theory of open systems in physics and biology. *Science*, 1960, **111**:23-28.

3. Richter, C. P. Behavioral regulation of homeostasis. *Symposium on Stress.* Washington, D. C.: Walter Reed Army Medical Center (WRAMC), 1953, 77-88.

4. Jackson, D. D. The role of the individual. *Proceedings of the Conference on Mental Health and the Idea of Mankind.* Chicago, February 1964.

5. Wallace, A. F. C. Mazeway distintegration: the individual's perception of socio-cultural disorganization. *Hum Organ*, Summer 1957, **16**:23-27.

6. Vickers, G. The psychology of policy making and social change. *Brit J Psychiat*, 1964, **110**:465-477.

7. Paul, B. D. (Ed.) *Health, culture and community.* New York: Russell Sage Foundation, 1955.

8. Ruesch, J. Social psychiatry. *Arch Gen Psychiat*, 1965, **12**:501-509.

9. Klein, D. C. The community and mental health: an attempt at a conceptual framework. *Community Ment Health J*, 1965, **1**:301-308.

10. Smith, W. G. & Hansell, N. Territorial evaluation of mental health services. *Community Ment Health J,* Summer 1967, **3:**119-124.

REPORT TWO

11. Reiff, R. & Reissman, F. The indigenous nonprofessional. *Community Ment Health J* (Monograph 1), 1965.
12. Caplan, G. *Principles of preventive psychiatry.* New York: Basic Books, 1964, 26-55.
13. Lindemann, E. Symptomatology and management of acute grief. *Amer J Psychiat,* September 1944, **101:** 141-148.
14. Gruenberg, E. M. The social breakdown syndrome—some origins. *Amer J Psychiat,* June 1967, **123:**1481-1489.
15. Peculunis, L. Department of Psychology, Northern Illinois University, DeKalb 60115, has current information on the curriculum and scope of the program.

REPORT THREE

16. Grinker, R. R., Sr. & Grinker, R. R., Jr. Mentally healthy young males (homoclites). *Arch Gen Psychiat,* 1962, **6:**405-453.
17. Sidle, A., Adam, J. & Cady, P. Development of a coping scale. *Arch Gen Psychiat,* 1969, **20:**226-232.
18. Wallace, A. F. C. *Culture and Personality.* New York: Random House, 1961, 84-200.
19. Wallace, A. F. C. Stress and rapid personality changes. *Int Rec Med Gen Pract Clin,* 1956, **169:**761-774.
20. Wallace, A. F. C. A biocultural theory of schizophrenia. *Int Rec Med Gen Pract Clin,* November 1960, **173:** 700-714.
21. Wallace, A. F. C. Mazeway resynthesis: a biocultural theory of religious inspiration. *Trans NY Acad Sci* (Series 2), May 1956, **18:**626-638.
22. Wallace, A. F. C. Mazeway disintegration: the individ-

ual's perception of socio-cultural disorganization. *Hum Org*, Summer 1957, **16**:23-27.

23. Speigel, J. P. Psychological transactions in situations of acute stress. *Symposium on Stress*. Washington, D. C.: Walter Reed Army Medical Center, (WRAMC), 1953, 103-112.

24. Tyhurst, J. S. The role of transition states, including disasters, in mental illness. *Symposium on Social and Preventive Psychiatry*. Washington, D. C.: Walter Reed Army Institute of Research (WRAIR), 1957, 149-172.

25. Carlson, H. B. The relationship of the acute confusional state to ego development. *Int J Psychoanal*, 1961, **42**:517-536.

26. Visotsky, H. M., Hamburg, D. A., Goss, M. E. & Lebovitts, B. Z. Coping behavior under extreme stress. *Arch Gen Psychiat*, November 1961, **5**:423-448

27. Naftali, A. The role of brain-images in social adaptation. *Int J Soc Psychiat*, 1964, **10**:30-36.

28. Hansell, N. Casualty management method: an aspect of mental health technology in transition. *Arch Gen Psychiat*, September 1968, **19**:281-289.

29. Bowlby, J. Separation anxiety. *Int J Psychoanal*, 1960, **41**:1-25.

30. Bowlby, J. The processes of mourning. *Int J Psychoanal*, 1961, **42**:317-340.

31. Lindemann, E. Symptomatology and management of acute grief. *Amer J Psychiat*, September 1944, **101**:141-148.

32. White, R. B. Motivation reconsidered: the concept of competence. *Psychol Rev*, 1959, **66**:297-333.

33. Skinner, B. F. *Science and human behavior*. New York: Macmillan, 1963, 227-333.

34. Ruesch, J. & Brodsky, C. M. The concept of social disability. *Arch Gen Psychiat*, 1968, **19**:394-403.

35. Glass, A. J. Psychotherapy in the combat zone. *Symposium on Stress*. Washington, D. C.: Walter Reed Army Medical Center (WRAMC), 1953, 284-294.

36. Glass, A. J. Principles of combat psychiatry. *Milit Med*, 1955, **117**:27-33.

REPORT FOUR

37. Gruenberg, E. M. The social breakdown syndrome: some origins. *Amer J Psychiat,* June 1967, **123**:1481-1489.
38. Goffman, E. *Asylums.* Garden City, N. Y.: Doubleday, 1961.
39. Appleby, L. Evaluation of treatment methods for chronic schizophrenia. *Arch Gen Psychiat,* 1963, **8**:24-37.
40. Galioni, E. F., Adams, F. H. & Tallman, F. F. Intensive treatment of back-ward patients. *Amer J Psychiat,* 1953, **109**:576-583.
41. Zusman, J. Some explanations of the changing appearance of psychotic patients. In Gruenberg, E. M. (Ed.), *Evaluating the effectiveness of community mental health services.* New York: Milbank Memorial Fund, 1966, 363-394.
42. Ludwig, A. M. & Farrelly, F. The code of chronicity. *Arch Gen Psychiat,* December 1966, **15**:562-568.
43. Ludwig, A. M. & Farrelly, F. The weapons of insanity. *Amer J Psychother,* October 1967, **21**:737-749.
44. Benson, M. *Community return service: procedures and forms pack.* Rockford, Ill.: H. Douglas Singer Zone Center, 1969.
45. Tyhurst, J. S. The role of transition states, including disasters, in mental illness. *Symposium on Social and Preventive Psychiatry.* Washington, D. C.: Walter Reed Army Institute of Research (WRAIR), 1957, 149-172.
46. Propst, R. Relationship of psychiatric halfway houses to other local services. Paper presented at the meeting of the National Institute of Halfway Houses, Chicago, 1963.
47. Freeman, H. E. & Simmons, O. G. *The mental patient comes home.* New York: John Wiley, 1963.
48. Caplan, R. *Psychiatry and the community in nineteenth-century America.* New York: Basic Books, 1969, Chapters 1, 3, 24 and 26.
49. Wright, A. B. Tent life for the demented and uncleanly. *Amer J Insan,* 1902, **59**:315-319.
50. Wilsey, O. J. Tent life for the insane. *Amer J Insan,* 1903, **60**:629-635.

INDEX